Any book written by a highly educated t   ...s might be easily passed over on the pretty safe assun.ption that such a tome would be a stodgy read at best. In the case of *Old Men of the Bible*, that would be an unfortunate mistake. Skip this fine book by Lindvall, Wansink, and Lawing and you miss out on an insightful and surprisingly humorous book on a difficult topic. Cormac McCarthy said this dangerous modern era is *No Country for Old Men*. Actually old age is no country for old men. The three bright chaps who wrote this excellent book have taken an unusual approach to the topic and the result is enjoyable and well worth reading. Unless of course you are not a male, do not know a male, and hope not to ever age beyond where you are right now.

—Mark Rutland
New York Times best-selling author of *David the Great*

Old Men of the Bible is a book written for anyone who wants to avoid the danger of not ending well. Packed with insight, humor, and anecdote, it's a really great read!

—George O. Wood
Chairman, World AG Fellowship
Springfield, MO

This is an outrageously good read. Interesting, engaging, and insightful. And so creative. You will never read the Bible the same way again. And if you never have read the Bible, this book might persuade you to dig in. Both God and the authors of this book have real senses of humor. I would like to see them in a storytelling contest.

—Quentin Schultze
Professor of Communication, Emeritus
Calvin University

Smyth & Helwys Publishing, Inc.
6316 Peake Road
Macon, Georgia 31210-3960
1-800-747-3016
©2019 by Terry Lindvall & Craig Wansink
All rights reserved.

Library of Congress Cataloging-in-Publication Data
Names: Lindvall, Terry, and Wansink, Craig, authors; Lawing, John, illustrator.
Title: Old men of the Bible / Terry Lindvall and Craig Wansink.
Description: Macon, GA : Smyth & Helwys Publishing, [2019] | Includes
bibliographical references.
Identifiers: LCCN 2019017370 | ISBN 9781641731478 (pbk. : alk. paper)
Subjects: LCSH: Men in the Bible. | Grace (Theology)--Biblical teaching.
Classification: LCC BS574.5 .L56 2019 | DDC 220.9/20811--dc23
LC record available at https://lccn.loc.gov/2019017370

OLD MEN OF THE BIBLE

REFLECTIONS ON FAITH & AGING

BY TERRY LINDVALL
& CRAIG WANSINK

April 2020

To Willie
who is a descendent of
Matthew, Jesus' first
CPA. Thanks

[signature]

CARTOONS BY **JOHN LAWING**

Also by Terry Lindvall

*God on the Big Screen: A History of Prayers in
Hollywood Films from the Silent Films to Today*

*Divine Film Comedies:
Biblical Narratives and Sub-Genres of Film Comedy*
(with Dennis Bounds and Chris Lindvall)

*God Mocks: A History of Religious Satire
from the Hebrew Prophets to Stephen Colbert*

A Mirror for Fools: An Illustrated Alphabet of Religion and Satire
(with John Lawing, illustrator)

The Girl Who Couldn't Laugh (with Caroline Lindvall)

Surprised by Laughter: The Comic World of C. S. Lewis, revised

Celluloid Sermons: Emergence of the Christian Film Industry
(with Andrew Quicke)

Sanctuary Cinema: Origins of the Christian Film Industry

The Mother of All Laughter: Sarah and the Genesis of Comedy

*The Silents of God: Selected Issues and Documents
in Silent American Film and Religion, 1908–1926*

Also by Craig Wansink

Daily Dose of Knowledge: Bible

Chained in Christ: The Experience and Rhetoric of Paul's Imprisonment

Dedication

We three authors lovingly dedicate this work to our fathers,
John Lindvall, John Wansink, and John Vernon Lawing,
all like the beloved disciple John,
who grew very old, very loving, and very imaginative,

and to our sons,
Chris Lindvall, Teddy Wansink, and Reid and John V. Lawing III,
that they may grow up in the
stature and grace of their grandfathers.

Acknowledgments

I give thanks for my treelike wife, Karen, who has watched me grow old and yet maintained her youthful roots with music and mirth; my two untimely born kids, Chris and Caroline—with her freshly minted new husband Cary Joseph; and all my hearty old buddies with whom I laugh, mock, pray, argue, confess, and kvetch. To paraphrase C. S. Lewis, there is nothing as welcome and merry as the laughter of time-tested male friends, toasting God's goodness with a pint or glass of Divine libations left over from a Cana-like wedding and laughing with the One who guides us through the deserts and valleys. I also am hilariously grateful for the fresh women, Barbara Newington and Adelia "Dolly" Rasines, who breathe life, youth, and beauty into all they touch, for Frank and Aimee Batten Jr., who gave me a laughing place to grow old in, and for the amazing staff at Smyth & Helwys, especially the incomparable editor and overseer Leslie Andres, who made this project a delight.

— *Terry*

I am deeply grateful for the love, support, and grace of Nancy, the inspiration of Katrina and Teddy, the faith and family of Second Presbyterian Church, the enthusiasm of students and colleagues at Virginia Wesleyan, and the indulgence and good spirit of our colleague, Kelly Jackson.

—*Craig*

I offer my gratitude to my late father, J. Vernon Lawing, for his early interest in cartooning, and to my late mother, Flora Lawing, for a bitter sense of irony. From the work of cartoonist Cy Hungerford I learned that less can be more. For the small bits of biblical information that surface in my cartoons I am grateful to the faculties of Columbia International University and Gordon-Conwell Theological Seminary—not for the smallness but for their existence. And thanks for blessed children, John V. Lawing III, Reid Lawing, and Beth Banks. As always, I am grateful to the great G. K. Chesterton for helping me think logically and, finally, to my wife, Joan, who has the misguided idea that all my cartoons are funny.

—*John*

Contents

Foreword: Methuselah's Memory (AKA John Lawing's Memory)   ix

Introduction: The Grace of God   1

1: The Dirt of Adam   7

2: The Drinking of Noah   17

3: The Worry of Abraham   29

4: The Wrinkles of Isaac   41

5: The Tricks of Jacob   61

6: The Complaint of Moses   71

7: The Carnality of David   85

8: The Folly of Solomon   95

9: The Pride of Hezekiah   103

10: The Sharpness of Paul   111

Conclusion: The Grace of God Redux   119

Methuselah's Memory (AKA John Lawing's Memory)

My name is Methuselah. According to Bishop Ussher's questionable dating system, I was born in the year 167 and lived to be the oldest man in the Bible. The authors of this mish mosh have, like the witch of Endor, summoned me from the other side to offer its readers this introduction.

There are at least two notable things about the list of elders in this book. The first is that there are no Goyim in it. The second is that I am not in it. These things probably say a lot, but I'm not sure what. On the first point, it may say that Jews live longer than Goyim or that they keep better records. On the second point, the young schlumps responsible for this schtuss say my presence would be too expected. What am I—an unborn baby? But then I am used to insults. It was Mr. Gershwin who asked the question, "But who calls dat livin' when no gal will give in to no man what's nine hundred years?"[1] So I'm content to take the role given me and offer you this introduction.

What is the purpose of this book?

Will it give you a deeper understanding of the Scriptures?

No.

Will it help you explore the meaning of life?

Definitely not.

Will it help you to avoid the pitfalls of these schmendricks?

Probably not.

Will it give you a recipe for great matzo balls?

Definitely not.

Is it the one volume you should have if stranded on a desert island?

No. On a desert island, better you should have a copy of *Thomas' Guide to Practical Shipbuilding*. (Mr. Chesterton sends his regards. He's lost a lot of weight.)

What, then, will this volume do? Hopefully it will provide you with a few chuckles and its authors with a few shekels, and if it directs you back to the Original Source to see how far the authors have gone astray, so much the better.

Well. I'm back to the other side. Shalom.

—Methuselah

Note

1. "It ain't necessarily so," music by George Gershwin; lyrics by Ira Gershwin. The song comes from the Gershwins' opera *Porgy and Bess* (1935).

The Grace of God

As we three old professors with seminary education—Craig Wansink, Terry Lindvall, and John Lawing—gathered to ruminate upon some old men in the Bible and reflect upon aging, never knowing when our time might be up. It wasn't quite a morbid thought. Monks during the Middle Ages would sleep in coffins to come to grips with the transitory nature of this life. How quickly time passes, and we don't realize it.

In France in the seventeenth century, life expectancy was about thirty years. A teenager had about a 50 percent chance of making it to age fifty, 25 percent of making it to sixty-five. Thus, if anyone made it to seventy, he was considered a sage, with old age being the crowning achievement of an exceptional life. Life tables recording human longevity showed that one better get one's life in order quite early. Cynthia Skenazi looked at the essays on aging by Michel de Montaigne, who wrote in the 1500s that we learn too late not to dawdle with education and apprenticeship and need to get to early accomplishment, for mental and physical decrepitude will come soon enough. He scribbled that "I would rather be old for a shorter time than be old before my time." He saw that one of the benefits of old age was that God favorably allows us to die by degrees; "the last death will be so much the less painful; it will kill but a half or a quarter of a man."[1] (The other delight is that whoever sees old age can applaud the past and condemn the present age. You have the privilege of becoming a curmudgeon.) The danger of old age is that it might wrinkle your spirit even more than your face. Montaigne wrote elsewhere,

> I hold it as certain that since that age [thirty], my mind and my body have rather shrunk than grown, and gone backward rather than forward. It is possible that in those who employ their time

well, knowledge and experience grow with living; but vivacity, quickness, firmness and other qualities much more our own, more important and essential, wither and languish.[2]

We suspect that some sanctified saints may protest our original title, *Old Men of the Bible: We're Not Getting Better; We're Getting Older*, but it is not intended to provoke or frustrate those who are improving physically, morally, spiritually, intellectually, and even sexually. Emerging sanctified people can easily find more suitable reading. We are simply looking at some old men and realizing that in many respects they really didn't become better men. And that we often feel like we are in their company, much too comfortably.

We know that women may not like this either, but the facts may speak more loudly than their protests. The facts may turn some men toward the hope of getting better. We may be saved by faith in the righteousness of God, but the Scriptures also advise us to do good works. When our friend George married a girl from Massachusetts, he came to realize that the way God worked in his life to improve him was by giving him the Holy Spirit with a Boston accent. No doubt, women seek to train their husbands in the ways that they should grow older and better. It is a lifetime goal. No doubt, however, men have amazing powers of passive resistance.

We are to improve, but the stories in this book are reminders that none of us escape being selfish, lustful, bitter, petty, or boastful. Such sins endure. Other sins pop up and surprise us by their ferocity. However, one of the great differences about old men who seek God is that they recognize and confess that they are as miserable as sinners in the geriatric ward as they were in middle school. That recognition may be a revelation of hope.

One other anecdote of a married couple may suffice. (We have found that many jokes and tales are basically parables with a comic twist.) The wife complained that the husband watched too much football on television and didn't really listen to her. So he muted the program and turned and faced her to listen to what she had to say. After a few sentences, she threw up her hands and exclaimed, "You still don't care!" He responded abjectly, "I'm listening! Do I have to care too?"

The focus of this book is hopefully greater and deeper than it might seem. It is all about grace—grace that saves, grace that redeems, grace that tries to make us better. But it is the grace of God in and through Jesus Christ.

Now, to change from plural voice to singular, the real theme goes back to one of my days at Fuller Theological Seminary in Pasadena, California, where I, Terry, met a lot of great old men. Some, like George Eldon Ladd, who would amaze us in class (especially when he made the Blessed Hope a present reality), would often turn up waxing eloquent, but also sad and drunk. He still blessed us with hope. Others, like Lewis Smedes, led us on quests for religious certainty as we sat in his small, cozy study in golden sessions that never seemed to end, yet he would confess to depression and wonder where God was. (However, he once acknowledged that God was with his wife, Doris, and would always appear at dinnertime.) He taught us quietly about forgiveness, demonstrating that no matter how old one got, one would still have opportunity to practice it. That wonderfully ancient Swiss theologian Karl Barth told the story about Pablo Casals, who, at the age of ninety, still practiced his cello four or five hours each day. When asked why he did this, Casals answered, "Because I have the impression I am making progress." Thus, we impudent students began to practice forgiveness, especially as we needed it so much ourselves.

But the saintly professor who resonated most and made us want to be better students, better scholars, and better men was Fuller's president, David Allen Hubbard.

I took his classes on Wisdom literature, and he would talk about his ill wife with such affection and poignancy and humor that our throats would clog with emotion. And the fact that a generation raised on the satirical magazine *The Wittenberg Door* would get choked up over some Hebrew proverbs and psalms (and a little bit of sex in Solomon's songs) was a testimony to Hubbard's own poetic holiness.

It was the final sermon I heard from him that has stuck with me to this day. At Fuller's Baccalaureate in May 1973, as we cheeky master of divinity pups were about to embark and leave the modest Pasadena campus (no more Rose Parades), Hubbard stepped up to the podium in the First Presbyterian Church on Colorado Boulevard and spoke to us from three verses in Paul's letter to the Ephesians.

From the beginning, he read, "Paul, an apostle of Christ Jesus . . . . Grace to you and peace from God our Father and the Lord Jesus Christ" (1:1-2).

And then, jumping to the middle, he continued, "For by grace you have been saved though faith, and that not of yourselves; it is the gift of God; not as a result of works, that no one should boast" (2:8-9, NAS).

Finally, he turned to the last verse of the epistle and concluded, "Grace be with all those who love our Lord Jesus Christ with a love incorruptible" (6:24).

With these three verses he set out his theme: "Grace in the beginning. Grace at the end. And Grace all the way through."

It was an idea that not only would sustain us tiptoeing into our world but also would form a foundation of the gospel for the rest of our lives.

"Grace in the beginning. Grace at the end. And Grace all the way through."

This is our theme as we wade through the sketchy stories of the old men of the Bible, becoming acquainted with great patriarchs from Adam to the Apostle Paul. They failed in many ways, yet what sustained them and gave them their anchor was the grace and providence of God working in and through them, not as a result of their works, but as it pleased God. We are glad the writers of the Scriptures kept these stories in the Bible, even though they don't present a tidy prosperity message.

The old men needed grace at the end, just as they needed it in the beginning and all the way through. It is a wonderful realization that all along, the grace of our Lord Jesus Christ keeps us and does not fail.

"Grace in the beginning. Grace at the end. And Grace all the way through."

No matter how messed up we get. Or how old.

Notes

1. Michel de Montaigne, "Of Experience," in *The Complete Essays of Montaigne*, trans. Donald M. Frame (Stanford: Stanford University Press, 1958) 845.

2. Montaigne, "Of Age," ibid., 238.

Chapter 1

The Dirt of Adam

I first met John Lawing more than forty years ago, a long time in a wilderness, when he was already forty-eight years old. He had been a North Carolinian journalist, a cartoonist for *Christianity Today*, and other sundry things, but he was to become my best friend at Regent (nee CBN) University in 1978 when we met to start a graduate school of communication, with no students, no buildings, no syllabi, and no idea of what we were doing.

He was, as one of his students called him then, "old as dirt." He hasn't gotten any younger.

But we might as well start before that, at the beginning of it all— as John would remind me that we were all related to the Old Adam (about 6,022 years old next April 1 according to Irish Primate Bishop James Ussher). Adam has lived in our bones since we were born, and we share his dust to the day we last breathe.

Here was dirt older than John Lawing. Our former boss, the chancellor, president, and self-described "benign tyrant" of the school, Pat Robertson, was even older, even though he was the same age as John. Pat called John the university's "boy cartoonist," which suggested his enduring youthfulness. He called me "Peck's bad boy," an early-twentieth-century allusion that was Pat's equivalent of suggesting that I was a mischievous prankster on the level of a Bart Simpson. His reference merely showed how old he was even back in 1978. But then, as juvenile professors, John Lawing and I did throw snowballs at the dean's window and break it. At the first graduation ceremony, Robertson proclaimed that the graduate school of communication would train up a legion of journalists who would explain what the eruption of Mount St. Helens meant for the kingdom of God. John, the only journalist on the faculty, turned to me and asked, "What the hell does the eruption of Mount St. Helens mean for the kingdom of God?"

Biographically, we don't have much data on Adam, this man of the earth. Even his name suggests he was a representative of all humanity.

He could find no suitable companion among all the beasts of the fields, although he may have felt fondly toward the sloth. He was half of God's image, presumably not the better half. After falling asleep, he discovered upon waking to be less than when he fell asleep. He had lost an essential part of himself, but he now had it much better. Or so his new wife ribbed him.

In the dramatic story of Genesis 2, the individual Adam emerges. So we begin with our old man, with Adam, whose name in Hebrew meant "the human." According to the creation narrative of Genesis, he was the first man. However, the word's etymological Semitic roots also point to the meanings of clay, earth, ground, humus. We are related to the dust of the earth that the Creator breathed into, making the inorganic organic and making that amazing oxymoron, a spiritual animal, related on one side to the angels, the transcendent, the Amish, and on the other side to the donkeys, weasels, skunks, and religious studies professors.

God takes humus and dust of the ground and breathes into its nostrils (supposedly two holes in a proboscis-shaped part of the clay) "the breath of life" so that the creature becomes a "living soul."

Placed in an Edenic garden, where God had proclaimed everything "good," Adam wanders around naming things. However, such a task can become monotonous. God recognizes that of all the good things he has created, there is one condition that is not good, one joke that is not yet good enough to perform: "It is not good," God rumbles, "that man should be alone." The need to find a suitable companion begins. "How about a dog?" suggests God to a fellow who might be dyslexic.

"How about a cat? A mockingbird? A worm? A pachyderm? A mosquito?"

"Anything but the cat," says Adam.

Weary from his decision making, Adam falls into a deep sleep. God takes that particular bone from his side and forms a woman, named Eve, divinely attractive and frustratingly different.

However, before the woman appeared, God had warned Adam that while he could nibble on any fruit from the trees in the garden, there was one that he must avoid at all costs. God, in effect, said, "Do not eat from the tree of the knowledge of good and evil. Do not even think about chewing on ethics. For the day that you eat of it, you shall surely die. You may know all about good and evil, but you will no longer know Me. And as I am the only source of life, being cut off from me unfortunately means death. The fruit will make you old before your time and cause you to decay. Your only friend will be the worm."

The interdiction, the warning, carried its own consequences, like an apple falling on Newton's head. Like a fairy tale or myth, this story cautioned with a condition. "Don't open the box, Pandora." "Don't look at your husband, Psyche." "Don't eat the fruit, Adam." If you do . . .

British author G. K. Chesterton called it the "Doctrine of Conditional Joy." If you want a life of joy and peace, avoid this one mistake. God's one simple condition was to obey the word, and we blew it.

Mostly we know Adam as the one who disobeyed God when he was still young. Commanded not to eat of the fruit from the tree of knowledge of good and evil, he followed his wife, Eve, and did what he knew he ought not to. His sin made him as good as dead. And it made him old before his time. He lost his personal knowledge of God and picked up the habit of ethics, of knowing good and evil. It didn't take long for him to realize this had been a bad trade.

Adam aged faster than anyone who has ever lived upon the earth. He was eternally young one moment, and one bite later he had a foot in the grave. No liminal state. Just youth and then old age. Sin aged him. The smudge of sin worries us, wrinkles us, ruins us, and makes us weary with care. Finally, it kills us. Some of learn too late that what we eat may keep us up all night.

Chesterton, again, once observed that we get old while God remains eternally young, not by simply being outside of time but by being full of the vigor and vitality of youth. The large Fleet Street journalist wrote,

Because children have abounding vitality, because they are in spirit fierce and free, therefore they want things repeated and unchanged. They always say, "Do it again"; and the grown-up person does it again until he is nearly dead. For grown-up people are not strong enough to exult in monotony. But perhaps God is strong enough to exult in monotony. It is possible that God says every morning, "Do it again" to the sun; and every evening, "Do it again" to the moon. It may not be automatic necessity that makes all daisies alike; it may be that God makes every daisy separately, but has never got tired of making them. It may be that He has the eternal appetite of infancy; but we have sinned and grown old, and our Father is younger than we. The repetition in Nature may not be a mere recurrence; it may be a theatrical encore.[1]

Both John Milton and Mark Twain make the fall of Adam a more theatrical, even poignant, event. The Puritan writer of *Paradise Lost* put much of the blame on Eve as the disobedient one. Now, the word "obey" in the Greek means to put yourself under the hearing of, to listen. To disobey means not to listen. Thus obedience is not some military demand but a humble response to someone speaking to us. That's why when children disobey, parents might shout, "Are you listening to me?" Even in wedding vows, to obey might be a good thing to promise. *I promise to listen to you.*

In Milton's tale, Eve runs off for some time of her own, even before tempted by the serpent. This act of independence leads to her encounter with the snake, the ancestor of all moral philosophers and rhetoricians, not to mention advertisers, politicians, and lawyers. "You will be like God," the serpent promises.

Twain's excavation of the diaries of the two first beings aptly portrays Adam as a numbskull and Eve as the organized, intelligent one who assumes the responsibility of naming the animals.

Some wrongly connect the original temptation as sexual, as if the two had been celibate and only after their disobedience discovered their libido and then had to choose between God and a good time. But the pair is told to be fruitful and multiply before the fall. Sex was not the problem. It was a gift like good digestion and laughter, all of which would be ruined by a forbidden appetizer.

Cartoons of Adam and Eve after the expulsion from the garden often focus on their wearing fig leaves, a comic image exploited by Cardinal Carafa's censorship of Michelangelo's nude painting on the ceiling of the Sistine Chapel. Those leaves were pasted on strategically to conceal the naughty bits. However, cartoons may also show Eve picking up leaves and complaining that Adam doesn't put his clothes away. Or Adam stopping Eve from eating his dirty laundry as her salad. Cartoons also show them blaming one another, a habit that continues to this day.

The oldest joke came about after the fall when Adam had to order some trousers from a Jewish tailor. When it took so long, Adam complained, "God made the universe in seven days and it took you thirty days to make my pants." "Yes," answered the tailor, "but look at the world and now look at the trousers."

No, Adam and Eve fell because they wanted the knowledge of ethics. They could either know God personally or attain the knowledge of good and evil, without having the ability to obey that knowledge. Thus, they discovered two facts about all human existence: We know we should live in a certain way; none of us do live that way. We fail even in our own low expectations of an ethical life.

After beginning his eloquent dissertation on the resurrection of Christ in his letter to the Corinthians, the apostle Paul steps back a bit and reflects on why this young Savior was needed. First, he asserts that, "since by a man came death, by a man also came the resurrection of the dead. For as in Adam all die, so also in

Christ all will be made alive" (1 Cor 15:21-22).

The old man here becomes a metaphor for all human beings, who all disobey and die. Adam got old the moment he bit into the fruit of knowledge. Knowledge not only puffed him up but also wrinkled and aged him until he had nothing to look forward to but death.

The name "Adam" in its earliest use encompasses both male and female (gender nonspecific, as God's image combines the two and only later divides, which creates a host of challenges in trying to put male and female back together and keeping them there), with all humans (not just Adam) being created on the sixth day.

The story of Adam's aging is well known, as Eve is lured into a manipulative dialogue with a serpent. She is duped and—through a simple invitation—persuades Adam to join her. Disobeying Yahweh's command (not listening to it), the two sin and are expelled from Eden.

Perhaps what wearies Adam are God's rhetorical questions, "Where are you?" and "Why did you hide?" The query prompts Adam to examine his behavior and makes him aware that he did wrong and is now naked. However, he blames the offense on the woman and then on the Creator.

The Lord judges all. First, the serpent is to crawl, losing limbs of transportation and forced to eat dirt and die. Then the woman is to suffer the pangs of childbirth. Finally, the Lord punishes Adam by making his labors increasingly grueling and exhausting. Adam will be worn out with work; even the 9-to-5 routine will prove onerous and taxing, and the toilsome time will wear him out, especially if he becomes an actuary. The ground itself is now cursed and death comes to all. And in Adam's old age, one of his sons kills another. Cain, like many men of the Bible, had anger problems. But other issues mount.

As Martin Luther allegedly quipped, "Good God . . . what a lot of trouble there is in marriage! Adam has made a mess of our nature. Think of all the squabbles Adam and Eve must have had in the course of their nine hundred years. Eve would say 'You ate the apple' and Adam would retort 'You gave it to me!'"

The Hebrews used a chiasmus structure in their poetry that allowed two bits to parallel each other in an inverted way. Thus, the curse shows Adam that he will return to the ground, since he was taken from it; as he is made from dust, to dust he will return. What goes around will come around. The poetic justice of it all makes him realize that sin has made him old, as old as dirt. As Shakespeare quipped in *Cymbeline*, "Golden lads and girls all must, as chimney sweepers, come to dust" (Act IV, sc. 2).

Jewish pseudepigraphical writings, like the *Apocalypse of Moses* (aka *The Life of Adam and Eve*), follow the pair from the gates of the garden to their deaths. Mark Twain's *Diary of Adam and Eve* tweaks this story from the pair's own piquant and comic perspectives.

Yet Twain would mark the moment of the fall with dramatic images. Adam watches Eve as her disobedience shows immediate effects. Her hundred years of bliss are now exposed as "faded the heavens of her eyes and the tints of her young flesh, and touched her hair with gray, and traced faint sprays of wrinkles about her mouth and eyes, and shrunk her form, and dulled the satin luster of her skin."[2] Sin makes her old. And Adam takes the apple to grow old with her. He swallows hard, and his Adam's apple bulges so that with every bite he takes from then on, he will remember his fall.

What the Hebrew and Christian Scriptures point out clearly, however, is that Adam is our grandfather. He established a pattern for all who followed (Rom 5:14). Hosea, never known for his good luck with a wife, points out (Hos 6:7) that Adam broke the covenant. Hosea may have been quietly trying to figure out why Gomer went wild. Hosea and we know that we inherited Adam's genes, for weal and for woe. His nose is our nose. His sin is our sin. His problem with woman is the same.

Thus, the old greeting, "How's your old man?" becomes a theological question.

He's dead. The old man is dead. He bumped his head and he went to bed and didn't get up in the morning.

Former president Ronald Reagan remembered visiting a pub in Ireland (named after him) and passed through a local cemetery. His guide paused before one large tombstone that read, "Remember me as you pass by. For as you are, so once was I. And as I am, you too will be. So be content to follow me."

Some wary Irishman had scribbled on the grave, "To follow you I am content; if only I knew which way you went."

But good news always interrupts, unexpectedly. Another Adam will come along.

The new relation came through a Second Adam, the last Adam. While sin and death entered the world through the first Adam's offense, a fresh start is given in this last, ultimate, final Adam, One who sets it all right. The obedience of the final Adam enables life to abound to any who would receive it (Rom 5:12-19).

Adam couldn't resist the fruit. Jesus resisted every temptation thrown his way yet was without sin (Matt 4:1-11). The serpent said, "Take and eat" to Adam and to Jesus, "Make this stone into bread." The appetite of the first succumbed; the second triumphed. He did not eat but gave his own body to feed others.

Overcoming the temptations of Satan in the desert, Jesus prepared for the ultimate battle on the cross, where a duped Satan was tricked by his own superficial victory. Both Augustine and St. John Chrysostom saw the crucifixion as the grand joke played on the devil. Thinking he won with the inevitable defeat of the good, Satan was hoodwinked as God pulled a rabbit out of his hat in time for the first Easter and resurrected his own Son.

Through this primary transgression of one Adam, old age crashed down upon us and made us as destined to sin and death as he was. However, the apostle Paul argues that as "in Adam all die, so in Christ all will be made alive" (1 Cor 15:22). Paul reminds us that God's covenant with Adam represented the whole human race, but that covenant broke down. It didn't work.

Even though he was a "ruler of creation," Adam couldn't rule himself. So a new ruler of creation (Rev 3:14) was needed, one who could make all his people new creations (2 Cor 5:17).

God breathed into Adam the breath of life. Jesus breathed on his disciples and said, "Receive the Holy Spirit." With the first Adam, the human became a living being. With the second, one became transformed into a life-giving spirit.

The first Adam came from the dust. The second Adam came from heaven and took on the dust of flesh.

Two family portraits hang on our walls: First Adam and Last Adam. We do bear the likeness of those first humans, Adam and Eve. Yet, like in Dorian Gray's portrait, we can see too many similar flaws and smudges on the first. Like Oscar Wilde, we see ourselves as the ones who can resist everything but temptation. Like Oscar Wilde, we know the profound ugliness of our own heart's tendencies. Like Oscar Wilde, we see the selfish heart of the selfish giant in our breast. Like Oscar Wilde, we look at the blood on our hands and try to wash it out, only to muddy our own deaths.

According to the somewhat stubborn apostle Paul, we will bear the likeness of the Man from heaven at the resurrection of the dead. God will transform our dusty bodies so they will be like his glorious body. Death itself will be defeated, an enemy crushed under the feet of the final Adam. So, it was written, the first man Adam became a living being, but the last Adam a life-giving spirit. We move from the dust of the old earth to the glories of the new heavens and earth. "So shalt thou feed on Death that feeds on men," Shakespeare wrote in Sonnet 146. "And Death once dead, there's no more dying then."

But in this present moment, while we have been given the life-giving Spirit, we still retain the dust of the first Adam. We have not yet shaken the dust off our feet. It lingers. Sometimes it becomes mud. Not that we don't wash our feet daily or wash each other's feet in humility. But every day, they get dirty. And when these men of the Bible got older, some didn't wash their feet as much.

As William Lynch explained it, "The *mud in man* is nothing to be ashamed of. It can produce . . . the face of God. . . . To recall this, to recall this incredible relation between mud and God, is, in its own distant, adumbrating way, the function of comedy."[3] Using dust/dirt/mud/Adam, God is setting up a Divine Comedy. Someone is coming who will wash their feet, and ours.

For Discussion and Further Reflection

1. When you think of Adam, what stands out most about him? Do you think of anything not mentioned here?

2. What stood out to you in this chapter? What made Adam old? How does sin make you feel old?

3. Why did Adam have a desire to eat the fruit and be like God? Do you, in any respect, share a similar tendency?

4. Was Adam right to blame Eve for his predicament? How do you move beyond tendencies to blame others for your choices?

5. When Adam knew he was naked, why did he feel ashamed?

6. In a chapter on Adam, why is there so much description of Jesus? Describe the relationship between Adam and Jesus. What are ways in which we become better by reflecting on these?

Notes

1. G. K. Chesterton, "The Ethics of Elfland," in *The Everyman Chesterton*, ed. Ian Ker (Everyman's Library; New York: Knopf, 2011) 309.

2. Mark Twain, "Diaries Antedating the Flood," in *The Bible According to Mark Twain: Writings on Heaven, Eden, and the Flood*, ed. Howard Baetzhold and Joseph B. McCullough (Athens: University of Georgia Press, 1995) 66.

3. William Lynch, *Christ and Apollo: The Dimensions of Literary Imagination* (New York: Sheed and Ward, 1960) 110.

Chapter 2

The Drinking of Noah

After Adam dies, plenty of old people appear throughout Genesis. They live into the eight and nine hundreds, with birthday cakes supporting enough candles to cause an apocalyptic conflagration.

Enoch was one old man who seemed to get better. When he was a mere pup of 65 years, he sired his son Methuselah (who would attain the record of 969 years). Broken down, Methuselah's name comes out as *Selah*, meaning pause, stop, ponder, and think, and *Meth*, which means meth. Think about drugs. At that age, you might be on quite a few prescriptions. (*Methuselah* in Hebrew means "man of the dart, the spear, or the javelin," basically a man who could fight.)

Then the Scriptures tell us that Enoch walked with God for 300 years. And then "he was not, for God took him." My father used to say that the two spent so much time together, enjoying each other's conversations and kvetching, that one day God said, "Enoch, we're much closer to my house today. Why don't you come with me to heaven?" And so Enoch was gone, quietly slipping away, a much better man than any man in the Hebrew Bible because he walked with God. The book of Hebrews tells us that Enoch "pleased God." So why not bring him home for dinner, even a banquet?

Methuselah's grandson was called Noah, and he was one who was to bring comfort for the toilsome work of the hands of his relatives. The ground had been cursed since the disobedience of Adam, and man labored diligently against thorns and thistles. In the sweat of their faces, they ate their bread, and then died, back into the cursed ground themselves: dust you are and to dust you shall return.

With so much dirt and dust, one would think water would be a relief.

It is a rare church nursery that lacks a mural or picture of Noah's ark. Or books focusing on animals, a rainbow, Noah, and Mrs. Noah.

Or a large plastic boat with pairs of plastic animals that can be put inside the boat.

It is an even rarer church nursery that highlights the story that occurs in Genesis 6 before God approaches Noah. Or that discusses what happened in Genesis 9 after Noah leaves the ark. And it is no understatement that when we see the sons of God having sex with the daughters of humans (in Genesis 6), or when we see Noah drink so much alcohol that he is not only drunk but also unconscious (in Genesis 9), we yearn for the shelter of being back on the ark.

Noah first appears in Genesis as humanity's best hope. He and his family build an ark and then save themselves and many animals from the rising floodwaters. Eventually, they leave the ark (disembark?). But then the story of Noah takes an unusual turn and becomes dark. If Noah in general is presented as a hero of the Bible, then the final scene of his life may remind us that life can dramatically change as we age.

Before Noah is introduced in the Bible, all is not well. Genesis 6:1-4 presents the problem:

> When people began to multiply on the face of the ground, and daughters were born to them, the sons of God saw that they were fair; and they took wives for themselves of all that they chose. Then the LORD said, "My spirit shall not abide in mortals forever, for they are flesh; their days shall be one hundred and twenty years." The Nephilim were on the earth in those days—and also afterwards—when the sons of God went in to the daughters of humans, who bore children to them. These were the heroes that were of old, warriors of renown. (NRSV)

These "Nephilim" were the results of what happened "when the sons of God went in to the daughters of humans, who bore children to them." Reading about sex may make us uncomfortable, but reading about interspecies sex takes that discomfort to an entirely different level. These Nephilim elsewhere in the Bible are described as giants, and they are not to be understood as the intent of God's creation. Things have gone wrong.

Immediately after the Nephilim are born, God is sorry that he made humans, with their evil hearts and intense violence. Apologetic for having made humans, and with deep grief, God says, "I will blot out from the earth the human beings I have created."

And then Noah appears in the story. When he is first mentioned, he apparently is about 600 years old.

Although God's intention is to wipe out all humans and life, that intent becomes narrowed when we are told that "Noah found favor" in the sight of the Lord and that he was "a righteous man, blameless in his generation; Noah walked with God" (Gen 6:9).

We know little about Noah, his character, his looks, or his life. What matters is that he was "a righteous man, blameless in his generation." Later rabbis would debate what Noah's being "blameless in his generation" meant. After all, it initially had been God's plan to wipe out every single person from the earth. So maybe, as Rabbi Yochanan argues in the Talmud, considering how sin-infused his generation was, Noah was blameless . . . relatively speaking.

Decades ago when we were young, and whenever talk became serious and turned to discussion of hell, it seemed like most of the people we knew hoped that God graded on the curve since, even though things weren't all that great in our lives, relatively speaking we didn't think we were as bad as others. Similarly, as the rabbis said, maybe Noah's integrity wasn't pure, but if we knew Noah's generation, he looked fantastic.

Sometimes the best we hope for is relative integrity. There were two brothers, well known in their small town for being crooked, mean, and nasty. When one of the brothers died, the surviving brother called the town's priest and said, "I'll give you $20,000 if, in eulogizing my brother, you call him a saint." The priest agreed. The whole town turned out for the funeral, and the priest began, "We always want to speak well about those who have passed on, but this man was a cheater, a thief, and a liar. He was mean, cantankerous, and ornery. However, compared to his brother, he was a saint."

But when the story of Noah begins, we don't know much about him except that God had decided not to wipe out all humans and that Noah was a righteous man. In addition, when he was about 500,

Noah beget his three sons: Shem, Ham, and Japheth. Begetting, as I told my church during one lectionary reading on genealogy, is all about sex. It's about reproduction, building up genealogies. Rabbits beget rabbits. Squirrels beget squirrels. Accountants may add, but few multiply.

What God saw was that the wickedness of man was great and the intent of the thoughts of their hearts were evil, *continually*. So God grieved; he repented that he had even made humans. He was so upset that he decided to exterminate not only humans but also every creeping thing, perhaps because he didn't see much difference between the corrupt creepy men and the creepy beasts.

But then, "Noah found grace in the eyes of the LORD."

What a great line. Grace in the beginning, grace in the end, and grace in the eyes of the Lord. The just and righteous Noah walked with God and pleased God, like his great-grandfather Enoch.

Finally, Noah was 600 years old when the floodwaters began to rise. Stuck with an overwhelming number of clean and unclean animals and birds—and those creeping things—Noah, his wife (who would become notorious during Miracle pageant plays in the Middle Ages as a nagging shrew who would not leave Noah alone), his three sons, and the sons' wives are to endure forty days and nights of rain, the kind one gets during a nor'easter. Every nostril on earth would be snuffed of breath. Only Noah and those on the ark would remain alive.

God warns Noah that humans are to be destroyed and then tells him to make a three-decked ark out of cypress wood. The 300-by-50-by-30-cubit structure is to have rooms and be entirely covered in pitch. Noah is told that he, his wife, his sons, and their wives are to come into the ark. So Noah takes his wife and his family on board.

Once, a minister placed his Bible on his pulpit, lying open to this passage in Genesis that he intended to quote during services. A mischievous boy, discovering the open Bible before church, glued two pages together. The minister, then, when he came to the Scripture text, read, "When Noah was one hundred and twenty years old, he took unto himself a wife, who was"—turn page—"one hundred forty cubits long, sixty cubits wide, built of gopher wood, and covered inside and out with pitch." The minister blinked, then said to his congregation, "I never came across this in the Bible before, but I accept it as evidence that we are fearfully and wonderfully made."

In addition, in the most visually memorable part of the story, Noah is told to bring two of every kind of living thing—both male and female—onto the ark (Gen 6:19). Five verses later, that is qualified when Noah is told, "Take with you seven pairs of all clean animals, the male and its mate; and a pair of the animals that are not clean, the male and its mate" (Gen 7:2).

This image of Noah and the ark is what so many of us imagine today. Many children in church grow up singing "Rise and Shine," which features such lyrics as "The Lord said to Noah: There's gonna be a floody, floody . . . The Lord told Noah to build him an arky, arky . . . He called for the animals, They came in by twosie, twosies, He called for the animals, They came in by twosie, twosies, Elephants and kangaroosie, roosies, children of the Lord."

Similarly, when we hear the story of Noah, we may think about art. If you look at paintings of the flood before our last century, the focus is not on the animals walking two by two up a gangplank (the two dogs, the two polar bears, the two giraffes). The focus is not on whether Noah allows—of course—the two termites on board the ship. The focus in these paintings is on what is happening outside the ship. Most people were outside the ark, at best looking through a porthole at the elephants and kangaroosie, roosies. Most people were drowning.

When the floodwaters came, Genesis 7:11 emphasizes that the waters came up from the earth as well as down from the heavens. Water was everywhere. In three verses, Genesis 7:21-23, we are told of the devastation. Every living thing on the earth is said to have died.

This is a difficult story to read. Focusing on a different Bible passage, there is a beautiful, Jewish Hasidic story that tells of a great celebration in heaven after the Israelites are delivered from the Egyptians at the Red Sea, and the Egyptian armies are drowned. The angels are cheering and dancing. Everyone in heaven is full of joy.

Then one of the angels asks the archangel Michael, "Where is God? Why isn't God here celebrating?" And Michael answers, "God is not here because He is off by Himself weeping. You see, many thousands of His children were drowned today."

It is difficult not to believe the same of God in response to the flood.

Noah's deliverance would finally come when he sent out a dove that returned with a freshly plucked olive leaf in her mouth, letting Noah know the waters had receded. When he sent out another, and it did not return, he prepared to disembark and urge all the confined beasts to be fruitful and multiply. Seemingly, after spending that much time on a forced Carnival Cruise, little urging was needed.

After an extended time, when the waters finally began to subside and when the face of the ground was drying, God commanded Noah to leave the ark. Perhaps Noah was eager to do so. Whatever else he experienced, it is hard to imagine the entire experience as being anything other than horrific.

When my family was young and took car trips, my overeager children would incessantly ask, "Are we there yet?" It was easy—even if we were barreling down the highway—to look in the backseat of the car, and say, "Yes. Get out." I said it jokingly, of course.

Whatever else Noah had experienced, he had been traveling with—and taking care of—an ark filled with animals. So Noah followed the command, left the ark, immediately built an altar to the Lord, and offered a sacrifice. God then blessed Noah and his family, and told them to "Be fruitful and multiply, and fill the earth" (9:1). God let them know that the whole vegetarian emphasis was in the past: "Every moving thing that lives shall be food for you, and just as I gave you the green plants, I give you everything" (9:3), but God was quick to acknowledge that the food did not include humans.

Then God established a covenant, emphasized that there would never be another flood to destroy the earth, and offered a bow—a rainbow—as a sign of that covenant. That would have been a wonderful place to end this story, but it does not end there. After the flood, when Noah and his family get off the ark, we want a happy ending. But almost immediately there are problems that take us off guard, first with Noah and then with one of his sons.

Now the weary Noah had done good. He built an altar to the Lord and offered burnt offerings (hopefully the clean animals had reproduced by this time), and the Lord received the soothing aroma. After forty days of stifling quarters, this smelled good. Although the Lord recognized that the imagination of the human heart is evil from youth, he promised that he would never again curse the ground. But to avoid the sin of Cain, God warned that whoever sheds a man's blood, by man his blood shall be shed.

For Noah, God established a fresh covenant, a promise for him and his descendants and with every creature (God always seemed concerned about animals, as he even allowed the cows in Nineveh to repent after Jonah preached). The covenant brought the rainbow, a sign of life and assurance never again to flood the earth to destroy all flesh.

Tired after a long cruise, Noah decided to become a farmer. As he got off the ark, he planted a vineyard. (That might cause us to raise an eyebrow.) He then got tipsy and apparently lay uncovered in his tent (9:20). (The eyebrow might continue to be raised.) Noah's son, Ham, then saw Noah naked and told his brothers. (Oh, that's not good.) Then Noah, when sober, cursed not Ham but Ham's descendants via his son Canaan.

NOAH, THE LORD MAY FIND YOU BLAMELESS BUT HE DOESN'T HAVE TO PICK UP AFTER YOU!

The first problem for Noah in his old age was drink. He drank too much and got drunk. For an old man, the blessings of wine for one's stomach and one's health are highly recommended. To paraphrase old Chesterton's quip, one should always drink when one is happy and when one is with friends, never when one is alone or sad. However, Noah was alone and didn't seem too happy.

The Bible goes further on the gift and the problem of drink. The first half of Proverbs 31 recommends that the one whose life is miserable should drink strong drink and forget his troubles. This passage occurs before the perfect wife is introduced. Maybe the poor sot got hammered because he had the most excellent of wives, 300 by 50 by 30 cubits, and fell far short of her stature. He had a Proverbs 31 wife who got up early and achieved manufacturing and real-estate deals before the husband opened one eye. She was amazing, and he didn't measure up. Thus, the book of wisdom, Solomon's *hokmuh*, advises readers to drink and forget your troubles.

One anecdotal story tells about Noah and his wife Naamah (daughter of Lamech and sister of Tubal-Cain and cousin to Fifi, who didn't quite make the trip) sitting on the deck of the ark after all the animals had left, drinking glasses of wine. Naamah whispers, "I love you. I couldn't have made it all these months if it hadn't been for you."

Noah pokes her and jokes, "Is that you or the wine speaking?"

She responds, "I was talking to the wine."

But Noah wasn't a happy drunk. With his hangover, he became an angry drunk. Poor Ham, stumbling upon his father's nakedness and possibly mocking him or at least gossiping to his brothers, got the curse of a forty-day-plus hangover. If Ham had had Instagram, the image of Noah might have gone viral. Shem and Japheth did the respectable thing, walking into the tent backwards and laying a garment over their father, not seeing his wrinkled old body.

When he woke from his stupor, he lashed out: "Cursed be Canaan (now the son of Ham); he shall be a servant of servants to his brothers." Even though one of his great-grandchildren would be the heroic one known as Nimrod, the mighty hunter, potentially one of the Avengers, Ham's kids had no chance. But Ham is the one who did what was wrong in the sight of his father.

A classic dad joke asks, "Why wasn't Noah's ark kosher?" The answer: "Because Ham was on it." And Ham is the problem here. It is unclear exactly what Ham did. In general, most interpreters see Ham's inappropriateness not in him seeing his drunken father naked per se, but in his telling his brothers rather than simply covering Noah and remaining silent. Philo, a Jewish philosopher from the first century AD, says that Ham must have "laughed at what he saw and proclaimed aloud what was right to leave untold." Ham was not sufficiently respectful and pious. He could have protected his father's honor, but he defamed him instead.

We know people today whose dispositions lead to defaming rather than supporting others. I love the story of Mildred, a church gossip who regularly inserted herself into other people's business. Because people feared her, they were not critical of her, but she made a mistake when she accused George, a new member of her church, of being an alcoholic after she saw his pickup truck parked in front of the town's only bar one afternoon. She commented to George and others that everyone seeing it there would know what he was doing. George said nothing, stared at her for a moment, and then walked away. He didn't explain, defend, or deny. He said nothing. Later that evening, George quietly parked his pickup in front of Mildred's house and left it there all night.

Originally, the story of Ham helped explain why the Canaanites, the enemies of Israel, were so evil. It was their nature. It was the way their descendant Ham behaved, so it is no wonder that they would do the same. But in the United States in the 1800s, people spoke of the curse of Ham or the curse of Canaan to justify racism and the enslavement of people of black African ancestry. They were said to have descended from Ham.

Here, the first curse in the Bible relegates the Canaanites to be the servants of the children of Shem, namely the Hebrews and the Greeks, who were probably descendants of Japheth. Noah's prayers for them are blessings that they may be served and be enlarged.

However else we may view this final story in the life of Noah, we must acknowledge that it is an ignoble ending to Noah's life—and not just because of how he is treated. We want our heroes of the Bible to leave the stage with more dignity. After the flood, we're celebrating with Noah, who survived, and the next thing we know he has planted a vineyard, drunk too much, and is like an unclothed Otis in the Mayberry Jail or like Foster Brooks on a Dean Martin Roast.

When Noah "awoke from his wine" (9:24), he cursed his young son, and then we are told, "after the flood Noah lived for 350 years" (9:28), dying at the age of 950, conveniently mnemonic ages.

What happened during his last 350 years? We don't know. This old man of the Bible aged. Not much else. And since many people of faith don't read the Bible, maybe Noah's reputation wasn't hurt all that much. After all, Fisher-Price's Noah's ark sells well, and church nurseries are covered with paintings of the ark and Noah.

We don't know much about Noah, but we do know that his story ends sadly. And although we are not offered much explanation of how and why his life became dark so quickly, Noah reminds us of what happens after a traumatic experience when we put our guard down, or when we fail to recognize the ways in which we are vulnerable, particularly through alcohol, drugs, television, or other escapes.

Did Noah's drinking result from the traumatic experience he endured? It would be surprising if it hadn't, particularly since it follows directly after the flood. The story of Noah is a reminder that all of us carry pain with us, and we respond to that pain in different ways at different times. It is a reminder that we need to care for each other and be gentle with each other. It is a reminder that each of us needs to be aware and vigilant of how our past has the power to overwhelm us.

And then we leave the rest to God.

For Discussion and Further Reflection

1. When you think of Noah, what stands out most about him? Is there anything not mentioned here?

2. What stood out to you in this chapter?

3. What do you make of Noah's drinking? Does it seem related to the flood? If not, is it a kind of character flaw? The book of Genesis did not need to share this story. Why do you think it was important to include it?

4. Are there ways in which traumatic experiences push you—or those you love—to alcohol, drugs, adultery, or other kinds of addictive behaviors?

5. Pain—particularly unresolved pain—can continue to shape and rule each of our lives long after the painful event. That trauma may come from broken relationships, the death of a loved one, or feelings of betrayal, injustice, or disrespect. How have you have seen friends deal with pain or trauma in unhealthy ways? How have they done so in healthy ways?

6. Reflect intently on ways in which you need to be aware and vigilant of the power of past negative experiences in your life.

Chapter 3

The Worry of Abraham

Abraham, the father of three faith traditions, obeyed when God called him to go to a place he had never heard of, a place that he was to inherit. God promised to bless him and make his name great. The Lord would bless those who blessed Abraham and curse those who cursed him. Through him all the families of the world would be blessed.

He left Ur of the Chaldeans to go to the land of Canaan when his name was simply Abram. He dwelt in this land of promise as in a foreign country, living in tents with his wife. He lived like a stranger in a strange land, living by faith and dying in faith.

Abram wandered until he came to the terebinth tree of Moreh, also known as the *pistacia palaestina* or *terebinthus* by botanists, who tidy up all trees and shrubs into helpful categories. Some call it an oak tree, full of shade and offering protection from the sun. The tree, in Hebrew known as *elah* (or, if you have many, *elot*), also appears in connection with idolatry and the worship of trees. For Freud, one's oak may be quite large . . . or quite small.

The tree's most famous appearance is in the Valley of Elah, or the Valley of the Terebinth, where David whacks Goliath with his little stone. But I digress.

Abram worried, and it seemed he had no reason to worry. He came from good stock and had amassed a fortune for his day. His life was full of adventure, leaving the idol-infested locale of Ur to travel toward some undisclosed promised land. God had tended him and Sarai, but the promise didn't seem forthcoming.

Because of a famine, Abram took his brood down to Egypt and there met up with the powerful king Abimelech, who obviously was quite taken with Abram's beautiful wife Sarai. This polytheistic king of Gerar, Abimelech, pops up three times in relation to the "she's my wife/she's my sister" vaudeville routine (twice by Abraham and once by Isaac). Abram beat out Henny Youngman by thousands of years with his line to the king, "Take my wife, please," pointing to the fact that men are cowards, even when you have conquered nations and overcome seemingly insurmountable obstacles.

Worried that the pharaoh might kill him, Abram persuaded Sarai to pretend to be his sister. The fact that she was related made it more than a mere lie. But Abram was trying to save his own skin, and this from a man who was to become a fearless warrior.

Taken to Pharaoh's palace, Sarai was exalted, and Abram didn't do too badly as Pharaoh showered him with sheep, oxen, male and female donkeys, male and female slaves, and, for fun, some camels.

But Abram knew this wasn't right. He worried a bit. God intervened and sent plagues upon the house of Pharaoh, who was bright enough to recognize his almost fatal mistake. "Why didn't you tell me she was your wife? Get out of here." Abram picked up his wife (and all the new belongings, probably loading up the convenient camels) and skedaddled out of Egypt.

The story doesn't puff up the reputation of Abram, but it does let us know how good-looking his wife is and how God provided special protection over his weak patriarchs and how Abram worried when he didn't need to.

With rich loads of goods and livestock, Abram returned to Canaan and would collect old jokes, like the one by George Burns: "People ask me what I'd most appreciate getting for my 87th birthday. I tell them, a paternity suit." But that was not merely a joke. Abram thought he would be happy with an actual paternity suit.

Throughout his life, Abram was a joke, basically a schlemiel. It seemed bad things happened to him, often. His nephew Lot was the schlimazel, a chronically unlucky man. He got first dibs on choosing what he thought would be the best real estate and took advantage of Abram's generosity. (Lot then came to his own ironic lot in watching his wife turn into salt; no longer could he pass the condiments without a wry regret.)

But it does seem that Abram's problem was the little weed of worry. All sins start small, and each time one surrenders to the sin, it grows a bit more, like the Baobabs on the Little Prince's planet.

In Antoine de Saint-Exupery's tale of *Le Petit Prince*, small sprouts, if untended, grow into mammoth vegetation that threatens to over-take the entire planet. What begins as a casual habit becomes an addiction. Each moment, we grow into the kind of person we are practicing to be. Worry would be that weed for Abram.

Later in his story, he would worry about the wicked city of Sodom and intercede for the town where Lot lived. He bartered with God, who had confided in Abraham (as his name was then) that he was about to destroy the city because the people's sin was gravely depraved. "But," pleaded Abraham, "will you also destroy the righteous? How about if there are fifty righteous within the city?"

"Okay," God conceded. "If you can find fifty, I will spare it."

Abraham realized the number may be too high. "How about forty-five, forty, thirty, twenty, ten?" The Lord gave in with each reduction, but alas, not even ten could be found.

All of Abraham's bartering was the fruit of his anxiety, his care about the world. Worry, like any other sin contracted in youth, will increase with compound interest. C. S. Lewis wrote that, as Christians who believe humans live forever, we must recognize that what matters "is those little marks or twists on the central, inside part of the soul which are going to turn it, in the long run, into a heavenly or a hellish creature."[1] Lewis reminded his readers that

> Christianity asserts that every individual human being is going to live forever, and this must be either true or false. Now there are a good many things which would not be worth bothering about if I were going to live only seventy years, but which I had better bother about very seriously if I am going to live forever. Perhaps my bad temper or my jealously are gradually getting worse—so gradually that the increase in seventy years will not be very noticeable. But it might be absolute hell in a million years: if Christianity is true, Hell is the precisely correct technical term for what it would be.[2]

Abram's little weed was worrying. He was competent in so many ways: even his men could take on any four or five kings and do damage. When his nephew Lot was abducted by foreign kings (the tall Rephaim and Emim, one king having a bed more than a dozen feet long [Deut 3:11], and we're talking about big feet), Abram armed his 318 trained servants and strategically attacked these kings, rescuing his captive relative and bringing back all of Lot's goods "as well as the women." Abram was a great military hero. Yet he was bothered by one little thing that would grow exponentially.

His problem in old age was his worry. Worry is when you eat your own bones. To fret means to gnaw, and you chew on your own soul, which is like eating air. It does no good. As Mark Twain wrote, "I am an old man and have a great many troubles, but most of them never happened."[3] It's like Erma Bombeck's rocking chair, giving you something to do but never getting you anywhere.

Each day we are turning one small sin or virtue into our character. Incrementally, the little act becomes a habit. Peccadillos mushroom into addictions.

God made a covenant with Abram and told him not to fear. But Abram must have looked at his present circumstances and queried something like, "What will you give me, seeing that I am childless and am stuck with old Eliezer of Damascus as my heir? You've given me no offspring!"

God showed him the stars of the heavens and asked if he could number them. "So shall your descendants be." Abram believed. Something about listening to God allayed his worries.

However, even after a sacrifice, Abram fell into a deep sleep and was overwhelmed by a great darkness and horror. God told him that his descendants would become strangers in a land that wasn't theirs for four hundred years. "But don't worry, they shall return and come out with great possessions."

Despite such assurance, worries reappeared as time passed.

Abram looked at the big shadows of little things. Regardless of God's promise, things looked grim. Close to age 100, he didn't have one kid. But rather than worry in his tent at Mamre, he asked Sarai his wife what to do. Having had enough of his constant fretting, she suggested he go fool around with her maidservant Hagar, an Egyptian.

Abram had worried over his wife quite a bit, whether she would have cuddled up with young King Abimelech. As an original patriarch, he had little power inside the home where the matriarch ruled. He may have been designated as head of the family, but as the saying goes, "The bride is the neck and she can turn the head any which way she wishes."[4]

It was not so much the sin as the sheer stupidity and folly of taking Sarai's suggestion to bed Hagar. Once again, he proved that old men are jokes. As the maxim from the Talmud points out, "If one man says to thee, thou are an ass, ignore him. However, if two men tell you that, go buy a saddle." Abram bought several saddles, just in case.

Once Hagar conceived, she looked condescendingly at her mistress. Trouble brewed with the women of Abram. "My wrong be upon you!" lamented Sarai to Abram, in effect saying, "You did what I only suggested. You should have known better."

When Abram celebrated his 99th birthday, he heard again that he would be a father, and he fell on his face. God reintroduced himself: "I am Almighty God." God announced that it was about time to change Abram's name to Abraham because he was going to make him a "father of many nations." The name Abram meant "Exalted Father." Now he was to be called Abraham, "Father of a Multitude." One suspects that Abraham fell down in awe, but what was to come would surprise him even more.

For God then told him that the sign of this covenant would be circumcision. This seems to be an added stipulation from the original covenant established a few chapters earlier. This external sign, in which the foreskin of the penis would be cut away, meant that Abraham would recognize that this promise didn't depend on his own ability. There would be no confidence in the flesh. There would be a bit of pain and suffering, but having a foreskin hadn't done him much good in begetting a kid for about half a century.

God looked at Abraham and said, "Give me some skin."

Abraham said, "Sure, God," and gave him a high five.

"No," said God, "a bit lower."

When a boy is eight days old and has no knowledge of what is about to happen, he shall be circumcised or cut off from the family inheritance (no pun intended).

The Greek word *peritome* should be one of the most frightening words a boy learns. For Jewish boys, like Paul nee Saul, a pun lurked in its meaning. When legalists tried to get everyone circumcised, Paul mocked them: "not just *peritome*, but *katatome.*" In other words, if you want to hold on to this sign of the covenant, I don't want just a little slack, but cut the whole darn thing off. Forget Freud's symbolic castration theory; this covenant ritual comes mighty close to an

actual gelding, neutering, emasculating. It makes sense that Abraham might worry a bit here.

God then declared that Sarai's name would be changed to Sarah, from "princess" to "princess of many," marked with an "h" to give it a sort of Southern charm. Curiously enough, Sarah is the only woman in the Hebrew Bible whose age is given.

Then Abraham fell on his face again, this time laughing. The sheer incongruity of a child born to a man who is 100 years old and a woman who is past her prime at 90 was incredible. One does not have to read doubt in Abraham's response here as much as simply laugh at the fact that no one had invented Viagra.

I've noticed how such cures for erectile dysfunction are advertised with images of men with graying temple and slim, attractive wives, as if the man were a mere mellow mushroom and she a stalk of celery. Curiously enough, psychological studies on body image suggest that men feel they are in much better shape and condition than they are, while women feel less attractive than they are. Perhaps it is because men don't look in the mirror that much or because they have a much more vivid imagination.

We do know that the first time Sarah heard that Abraham would impregnate her, she fell on her face laughing. This was more than incredulity. This was divine incongruity. "Will I have the pleasure of my old man in my 90s when I never had it in my 20s?" Sarah asked, grinning.

As the old Yiddish joke goes, Abraham came home late in the evening announcing again that they were to have a son. "Sarah, Sarah!" he exclaimed breathlessly, "God has promised us super sex!"

Sarah looked at his wrinkled old body and said, "At your age, take the soup."

Abraham trusted God that, at the ripe old age of 100, he might impregnate his younger old wife of 90, though he was, as the author of Hebrews describes him, as good as dead down there. He rose to the occasion and spread his descendants as many as the stars of the sky and as innumerable as the sand on the seashore. Still, the tactic of a husband coming home and announcing, "God wants us to have super sex," may be one that is underused.

Old age has a tremendous impact on happily married couples. According to Agatha Christie, the best husband a woman could have would be an archaeologist, because the older she gets, the more interested he is in her. Alexandre Dumas the Younger observed that "a woman whom one has watched growing old is never old." Staying married reveals more beauty in your spouse.

However, when God divided his image into male and female, he created a perpetual incongruity of two beings so divinely alike and so frustratingly different that humor must be the result. Mischief occurs between the two genders. In one story, an 80-year-old woman had to appear before a judge for shoplifting a can of peaches. When she went before the judge, he asked her, "What did you steal?" She replied, "A can of peaches." The judge asked her why she had stolen them, and she replied that it was for the thrill of it all. The judge asked her how many peaches were in the can. She replied, "Six." The judge said, "I will give you six hours in prison."

Before the judge could pronounce the punishment, the woman's husband spoke up and asked the judge if he could say something. "What is it?" the judge asked.

The husband said, "She also stole a can of peas."

When Isaac was finally born, Abraham had to worry about the bullying relations between Hagar's boy Ishmael and Sarah's Isaac. He sent his first son Ishmael away, but with the promise that God would watch over him.

Then God decided to test Abraham. Abraham was called to sacrifice his only son Isaac, whose name in Hebrew means "he laughs." Abraham obeyed the Lord, hiking up to the mount at Moriah.

Here, Abraham, the father of all laughter, almost lost his laughter. God said he wanted Abraham to kill his beloved laughter. In a society in which Molech, the Canaanite calf-headed deity to whom children were sacrificed alive, reigned supreme, this notion that God wanted Abraham to give up his son as a sacrifice was not an absurd joke; it was a cultural practice. With such an order, Abraham may have thought he did not know his Lord as well as he thought. Whatever angle one looked at it, Abraham did, however, climb Mount Moriah with—as Kierkegaard would put it—fear and trembling.

According to Woody Allen's parody of the sacred text, Abraham's wife Sarah grew vexed with her husband's credulity and asked, "How doth thou know it was the Lord and not, say, thy friend who loveth practical jokes, for the Lord hateth practical jokes and whosoever shall pull one shall be delivered into the hands of his enemies whether they pay the delivery charge or not."

And Abraham answered, "Because I know it was the Lord. It was a deep, resonant voice, well-modulated, and nobody in the desert can get a rumble in it like that."

At the last minute, in Allen's parody, the Lord stays Abraham's hand and asks, "How could thou doest such a thing?" Abraham confesses that he never knows when the Lord is kidding. And the Lord thunders, "No sense of humor; I can't believe it. It proves that some men will follow any order no matter how asinine as long as it comes from a resonant, well-modulated voice." And with that, the Lord bids Abraham get some rest and check back with him tomorrow.[5]

Abraham discovered that old jokes were as good as new ones—even better. He called the place of sacrifice "The Lord Will Provide," a confirmation that to trust in the Lord is better than to worry. He was learning to be anxious about nothing, casting his cares upon the Lord who sustained him.

The Lord did provide; he brought forth the goat—a sacrifice made for Isaac—and kept his promise. Later, God would offer his only Son up as a sacrifice.

And after all these things, Abraham and Sarah are never recorded as having spoken to each other again. Perhaps the chilling nature of a spouse's near execution of one's child led to the silence.

Finally, worry returned as Abraham grew anxious about getting his son the right kind of wife. Who hasn't prayed for their children to find the right mate? As we will see with one of Isaac's sons, we should worry in this area, or at least pray. Abraham was more deliberate. He didn't want to become Alfred "What, me worry?" Newman. That would have been chaos.

Planning does help to erase worry, but plans without divine intervention may go awry. But when Eliezer (who, now realizing he was not going to get the inheritance, was able to relax and obey his master and still get some cushy trips with all expenses paid) went hunting for a good wife for Isaac, the whole courtship had been set up by God. Rebekah was lingering at the well. She watered the servant's camels, offered him water, and announced to her parents that she was off to Canaan.

Finally, God promised Abraham that he would "go to [his] ancestors in peace and be buried at a good old age" (Gen 15:15). So, Abraham, at the end, did not worry. He believed, and it was counted to him as righteousness (Jas 2:23), and he was called a friend of God. How great! At the end of one's life, God looks down and says, "There's my friend—not always the brightest or bravest one, but the one I chose. And boy, could he make me laugh, especially when he worried."

It was some time later that God would address this problem specifically. Standing on the Mount, Jesus gave his sermon (a *sermo* in Greek means more like a chat, not a thirty-minute disputation or lecture) and advised his followers:

> Do not worry about your life, what you will eat or drink; or about your body, what you will wear. Is not life more important than food, and the body more important than clothes?
>
> Look at the birds of the air; they do not sow or reap or store away in barns, and yet your heavenly Father feeds them. Are you not much more valuable than they?
>
> Who of you by worrying can add a single hour to his life? Who can add a single inch to his height? And why do you worry about clothes? See how the lilies of the field grow. They do not labor or spin. Yet I tell you that not even Solomon in all his splendor was dressed like one of these. If that is how God clothes the grass of the field, which is here today and tomorrow is thrown into the fire, will he not much more clothe you, O you of little faith?
>
> So do not worry, saying, "What shall we eat?" or "What shall we drink?" or "What shall we wear?" For the pagans run after all these things, and your heavenly Father knows that you need them. But seek first his kingdom and his righteousness, and all these things will be given to you as well.
>
> Therefore do not worry about tomorrow, for tomorrow will worry about itself. Each day has enough trouble of its own. (Matt 6:25-34)

Abraham had his troubles, his worries, his concerns. But God had him, and that's what mattered.

For Discussion and Further Reflection

1. When you think of Abraham, what stands out most about him? Is there anything not mentioned here?

2. What stood out to you in this chapter?

3. Reflect on Abraham's relationships with Sarah, Lot, Hagar, Ishmael, and Isaac. Also think about his relationship with Pharaoh. What are the greatest challenges Abraham faced in terms of his character or choices?

4. Is Abraham's willingness to sacrifice Isaac troubling to you? Is that story supposed to be troubling to you? How are we to understand this story? Are you willing to sacrifice *anything* for God? Are you willing to sacrifice what means the most to you? When and where do you find these calls on your life?

5. A common poster reads, "Have you prayed about it as much as you have talked about it?" The quote reflects our tendency to talk and worry instead of responding to problems with faith, hope, and reliance on God. What do you worry about? Family, finances, faith? What are healthy ways in which you might address your own worries? Are there individuals you know who seem to handle worry well? How do they do so?

Notes

1. C. S. Lewis, *Mere Christianity* (New York: HarperCollins Digital Edition, 2009) loc. 171.

2. Ibid., loc. 114.

3. Mark Twain, quoted in *Bite-Size Twain: Wit and Wisdom from the Literary Legend*, comp. John P. Holms and Karin Baji (New York: St. Martins Press, 1998) 3.

4. Nia Vardalos, writer and actor, *My Big Fat Greek Wedding*, Gold Circle Films, 2002

5. Woody Allen, *Without Feathers* (New York: Ballentine Books, 1983) 26–27.

Chapter 4

The Wrinkles of Isaac

In Steve Harvey's popular program *Family Feud*, one expects unpredictable and comic answers to random questions. For example, when asked to name what old men tend to lose as they age, contestants offered telling responses.

The first answers focused on the physical: health, hair, teeth, muscle tone, physical fitness, sexual stamina, and, most ruefully, sexual opportunity. (Opportunity was valued much more highly than stamina. It doesn't do much good if you have the stamina but no opportunity.)

However, answers then became more personal and philosophical regarding what might be lost: friends, memory, money, life.

Ah, trouble comes to all. In his short animated film, *The Critic*, Mel Brooks plays an old man who attends an experimental film showing of abstract images on the screen. Throughout, he makes loud comments on the garbage he is watching. When told to shut up, he berates his fellow spectator. "I'm 86. I'm allowed to be loud. I'm going to die soon."

In real life in 1961, Brooks was recovering from surgery for gout and was working with Carl Reiner on a comedy sketch that involved the interview of a 2000-year-old man who described history as he saw it. In a Yiddish accent, the old man reminisces about the first language (basic Rock) and how Paul Revere was anti-Semitic because he yelled "all through the night, the Yiddish are coming, the Yiddish are coming!" The interviewer corrects him: "He was saying the British were coming." The 2000-year-old man simply responds, "Oh." Yet he points out that "As long as the world is turning and spinning, we're gonna be dizzy and we're gonna make mistakes."

Asked by an interviewer what is the hardest thing about aging, he reflects and slowly says, "It's empty spaces that used to be filled with all the people that you grew up with, the people you love, your family—they're all gone." The memories are sad.[1]

When we study Abraham's son, Isaac, the first issues about the infirmities of the body are important. Isaac's story is much less developed than that of either his father Abraham or his son Jacob. It is sketchy but significant, as he loses his hearing and his sight.

Fortunately, in contrast to the lives of his father Abraham and his son Jacob, Isaac's life was dull. Monotonous. Even as C. S. Lewis confided to *Time* magazine that an academic life is monotonous, he blurted, "I like monotony."[2]

There's nothing wrong with wanting some of the same old moments, the same diet, the same faithful and steady friends, the one wife of your youth. These are all good things and there's no need to change them. "I've had this tunic since I was 17, and it still fits." "I've had this car since I could drive." "I've had this wife since she captured me." "I've had this wart since birth." All comforting and reassuring bits.

Isaac started out being bullied by Ishmael, his stepbrother. He was almost sacrificed by his father, an acutely memorable event to say the least. He didn't go out to meet women himself, but his father's servant made a match for him. The eHarmony of his day was a servant named Eliezer. (Even though the founder of this online dating service was a Fuller Seminary psychology professor who launched the site in 2000. Dr. Neil Clark Warren sure didn't help us single theology students back in the early 1970s, but he may have looked at the new twenty-first-century crop of over-eager seminarians and realized he had a gold mine if he could work as a matchmaker.)

Isaac's middle life was quite uneventful, except for his arranged marriage with Rebekah and the almost simultaneous death of his mother, Sarah. They did have their honeymoon in her old tent. It's a bit creepy if you ask me, but traditions are traditions and Isaac was "comforted after his mother's death." Nothing like a honeymoon to help you forget a funeral.

Abraham had sent his servant Eliezer to find a suitable spouse for his boy. Eliezer, like many on a wife-seeking quest, ended up at a well, essentially the bar or popular dating app of the early biblical era.

One went to wells to quench one's thirst, to pick fights, and perhaps to pick up women. Jacob, Moses, and even Jesus met women at wells. And one of the shadier ones had had five husbands and was living with a man who wasn't her husband. Even she ended up with a drink of Living Water.

When Rebekah saw the camels coming, she asked the right question and won the bachelorette contest. She was remarkably canny. A strong, decisive, take-charge woman, she made decisions quickly. Isaac would have little chance to act like a patriarch. When she appeared on the horizon, he was simply sitting in a field, mooning over his life. He lifted his eyes and looked and, behold, camels were coming, and on one was this captivating woman. Her name, Rebekah, meant "tying or binding up." This woman would indeed captivate Isaac and tie up his heart, and he would love her.

As time passed, Rebekah bore Isaac two sons. The mother favored the younger one, Jacob, over the testosterone-charged Esau, the red, uber-masculine son. She began to manipulate her husband for the "lesser" one, Jacob.

Isaac still liked to eat—especially the game stew Esau cooked. Food and his infirmities would be his downfall. Rebekah whipped up some savory food that Isaac loved and then costumed her son Jacob in Esau's clothes, which were a little too big. With some goat skin on his hands and the smooth part of his neck, though, he could pass for his brother to his father.

The father felt the disguise and asked, "Are you really my son Esau?" Salivating over the steaming stew, he didn't recognize that Jacob lied: "I am." Isaac was a man eating, and nothing could interrupt a hearty meal, even conversation.

Isaac invited Jacob to kiss him and took the opportunity to smell the garments. Yeah, they smelled like a fertilized field; they stunk like Esau. So he blessed the wrong son, the deceptive son, the trickster.

"May God give you the fatness of the earth, and an abundance of grain and new wine," Isaac prayed, and then added the kicker: "May peoples serve you, and nations bow down to you. Be master of your brothers and may your mother's sons bow down to you." Finally, Isaac said, "cursed be those who curse you, and blessed be those who bless you."

Isaac had given his all to his devious son.

Once Jacob vacated the premises, Esau arrived with his own recipe for savory food. "Let my father arise and eat of his son's game, that you may bless me," he said.

That's when Isaac realized how old he was. He trembled violently. All his plans were come to naught. "Your brother came deceitfully," he said. Esau cried out bitterly, "Is he not accurately named Jacob, as he supplanted me two times, taking my birthright and my blessing?" From then on, Esau bore a grudge and plotted to kill his usurping brother. He would at least have the decency to wait for the days of mourning for his father to pass.

The sibling rivalry over the inheritance, the contesting of the will, brought grief to the old man, who couldn't distinguish his children anyway.

Two concerns haunt the aging of Isaac: first is his physical condition, and second is his mental and spiritual condition. In the first, he loses power over his body. In the second, he loses himself—even his name, laughter. Both are harbingers of old age.

As bodies fall apart, one loses touch. Going deaf and blind, probably cursed with a prostate as large as Mesopotamia, one sits and waits for worse things to happen. I have ears to hear, but I can't hear anything because of tinnitus. I've fallen and I can't get up. (According to the Centers for Disease Control and Prevention, many people over 65 are admitted to emergency rooms every year because of falls from slippery showers, throw rugs, and grandchildren's toys. And once one falls, one is more likely to fall again within a year.) Isaac was decrepit and not improving.

Isaac's life augurs one incredible curse of old age: we fall apart. We lose control of bodily functions and sensory abilities. The New Testament even has a prophecy that Peter would be led around when he got old (John 21:18). Jesus told him that when he was younger, he could dress himself and go where he wanted; when he became old, he would stretch out his hands, waiting for someone else to dress him and lead him where he did not want to go. At first, I thought that person would be his wife, but for Peter, it was probably the Roman authorities.

Isaac didn't have typical modern problems like carrying too much weight or dealing with smoking habits; diabetes was not an issue. But he got old and his sight and hearing declined. We might remember the stark candor of the young man to Father William in Lewis Carroll's *Alice's Adventures in Wonderland*:

> "You are old, Father William," the young man said,
> And your hair has become very white;
> And yet you incessantly stand on your head—
> Do you think, at your age, it is right?"[3]

Poor Isaac knew it wasn't right, but one has no choice amid the ravages of time. In Shakespeare's play about the seven ages of man, *As You Like It*, the last scene ends the strange, eventful history of man with a whimper rather than a roar. From being born as a mewling and puking infant, growing into a whining school boy with a shining

morning face, then becoming a sighing lover, a quarrelsome soldier, a just and fair man with a round belly and wise sayings, one wanders into the sixth overripe age and slips into pantaloons, spectacles on the nose, a pouch on the side (might it be a catheter?), and the big, manly voice turning again toward whistling, childish trebles.

Finally, being shaped by a second childishness and haunted by the omen of mere oblivion, the old man awaits his condition of being "Sans teeth, sans eyes, sans taste, sans everything" (Act II, sc. 7, line 166). From this world of a stage, the time for exit has come.

We come full circle, as Chesterton would observe, from being helpless, bald, drooling babies, kicking our legs in glee, to becoming helpless, bald, drooling old men, kicking the bucket in glee.[4]

Shakespeare's *King Lear* warns of how, at advanced age, "the wit is out." Knowledge is lost and one can't discriminate well; it makes sense that poor Isaac could not distinguish between his sons. The fool warns Lear that

> O sir! you are old;
> Nature in you stands on the very verge
> Of her confine: you should be rul'd and led
> By some discretion that discerns your state
> Better than you yourself. (Act II, sc. 4, lines 139–43)

Unfortunately for Isaac, the one who could have helped was Rebekah, but she was aligned with the trickster. As the old maxim goes, where women might not admit their ages, men will rarely act them. In one sense, both Lear and Isaac confess, "sir, I am too old to learn," and both pray not to be mocked. As Lear explains after his own erroneous judgment has brought folly down upon his head,

> I am a very foolish fond old man,
> Fourscore and upward, not an hour more or less;
> And, to deal plainly,
> I fear I am not in my perfect mind. (Act IV, sc. 7, lines 70–73)

According to the American Psychological Association, about 20 percent of Americans over 65 experience mental incapacity and depression, a process that lowers immunity and compromises one's ability to fight infections.[5] Exercise, social interaction, restorative sleep, and diet help. Isaac, we assume, had at least one of the three, with the healthy stews cooked by his family.

For many years, we try to keep the body under the discipline of the mind. However, as Shakespeare noted, "we ripe and ripe / And then . . . we rot and rot"[6] The body has a mind of its own. If we do not accept its slow decay, it will make a buffoon of us all. The body is God's temporary joke upon us, and if we do not accept that joke, we shall be made the greater fool.

In *The Rules and Exercises of Holy Dying*, Anglican cleric Jeremy Taylor's reflects on the bubble and vapors of life and how quickly the body decomposes. He observes how "teeth fall and die before us," a prologue to our own tragedy. Aging takes our "body in pieces, weakening some parts and loosing others; we taste the grave and the solemnities of our own funerals" by steps: "first, in those parts that ministered to vice; and next, in them that served for ornament; and in a short time, even they that served for necessity become useless, and entangled like the wheels of a broken clock. Baldness is but a dressing to our funerals, the proper ornament of mourning." Such is then followed by "gray hairs, rotten teeth, dim eyes, trembling joints, short breath, stiff limbs, wrinkled skin, short memory, decayed appetite."[7] The body falls apart. And it announces this fact in ways that are unseemly and comic.

Once, speaking to a group of elderly women, I mentioned that the body makes us into clowns, and they began to share and mock each other about their practice of "tilting," of quietly leaning to one side and letting breezes from the southern hemisphere escape into the ethereal world.

The fact that the body has expressions of its own, that it communicates with gas and emits sounds, shows us that we are not in control. We may lean to the right or lean to the left, but gas will escape as we tilt. Sometimes it might be worth confessing that we are "exhaustipated," basically too tired to give anything more than a fart.

One of the more common complaints among older people is constipation, signified by a bowel movement less than three times a week or straining a quarter of the time. My father-in-law identified a good bowel movement as one of the grand delights of old age. My academic colleague and friend, Dr. Eric Mazur, once told me about the five examples of constipation in the Hebrew Bible, besides Isaac sitting in the field meditating. First, Cain was not Abel. Second, Moses took two tablets down. Balaam couldn't move his ass. Samson brought the house down. And Solomon sat for forty years. One can have hope.

Another precious gift of old age that can be lost too easily is sleep. The psalmist celebrated that the Lord kisses his beloved, even in the beloved's sleep. It is a gift, especially for those who can't sleep. Many of us old men wake up with prostate pressures at least once a night. But the gift is getting back to sleep, or at least realizing that we will have a good nap the next day. To sleep, to snore, that is the quest. And we know we are old when "Getting any?" means "Getting any sleep?"

Writing when he was old, Shakespeare crafted one of his last plays, *The Tempest*, in which the old magician Prospero spoke about a positive image of aging. He offers a hopeful word that "our little [lives are] rounded with a sleep" (Act IV, sc. 1, lines 157–58), a most wonderful and tame view of death that the apostle Paul also uses (see 1 Cor 15:20). As Prospero reflects on the ending of his work, he acknowledges that he trusts in something more than himself and that such eternal sleep is a reward.

As we age, our sleep habits change. The great opportunity of being old is that one can practice Benjamin Franklin's "early to bed, early to rise" maxim. It also allows us to eat earlier in the evening and get happy hour prices for our food that we can then digest before we fall asleep at 8 pm.

However, some of us lose the ability to sleep deeply and be restored. We experience sleep fragmentation, waking up multiple times during the night, which, according to Bryce Mander and Joe Winer, sleep researchers at the University of California at Berkeley, may lead to depression, disease, and dementia.[8]

They emphasize that deep sleep offering restorative rest is important for good health, especially when it complements a healthy diet and exercise (for some of us, getting out of bed is an amazing feat of strength and will power). In turn, good food and regular exercise contribute to better-quality sleep. When asked, "Why do some people age more 'successfully' than others?" the researchers answered that better-quality sleep is one of the major factors. And it is the quality of sleep rather than the duration that helps the most.

Even with sleep, our bodies crumble, crack, leak, sag, and hurt. From bursitis in our shoulders to bunions on our feet to gastrointestinal problems, we are turned over to all the aches and pains that age is heir to.

In her book *Understanding Men's Passages*, Gail Sheehy argues that aging men have a harder time making a satisfying passage into the fourth quarter of their lives than most women. According to her, women may feel pangs over losing their youth, but men feel dread. They are about to lose their potency and their potential, feeling like actors on stage who have lost their voices. She writes that "Pharmaceutical companies are racing to offer men perpetual virility—by popping a pill. As immediate and compelling as is the concern most men have with how their sexual performance might be affected by getting older, there is much more involved in restoring vitality and virility than putting more lead back in the pencil."[9] Sheehy argues for the existence of male menopause.

Her greatest insight, however, may be that "Men don't understand women, but at least they know it. Women don't understand men, but they don't know it." I suspect that virility is not as much of an issue as mortality. Without a philosophy, or a theology, of change, a man stops in his tracks. Because most men are task oriented, they may not know what to do once the task is done. And many men do not discuss these things with other men. The male malaise is not shared; one goes at it alone. There is no country for old men.

Isaac had his boys and then all his grandchildren—more than he could have imagined. But he didn't know how to be a good grandfather unless, somehow, he could share laughter. I like to think Isaac could tell tales about his boys that made their kids laugh.

Over a century ago, a physician from Johns Hopkins University declared that cheerfulness and a rosy smile would conquer disease: "One of the most elemental proofs of convalescence in an invalid is his or her buoyancy, pleasure, and happy laughter."[10] His observation is akin to that in Mark Twain's description of an old man in *Tom Sawyer* who "laughed loud and joyously, shook up the details of his anatomy from head to foot, and ended by saying that such a laugh was money in a man's pocket because it cut down the doctor's bill like everything."[11]

One old wheeze of a joke concerns an older man who is walking down the street when he discovers a talking frog. The frog confides, "If you pick me up and kiss me, I'll turn into a beautiful woman."

The man picks up the frog and puts it into his pocket.

"Aren't you going to kiss me?" the frog complains. "I'll turn into a ravishing woman."

"I'd rather have a talking frog in my pocket," the old man says.

Isaac, whose name means "he laughs," discovered that laughter doesn't last. Laughter in old age is a blessing, but it's a rare one that, according to research, decreases significantly as one ages. The depressing part for some of our readers is that aging adults are defined as individuals who are sixty-five and older. You may not even be taking Social Security yet, but you are still defined as old.

Ageism, according to a recent article, has "deleterious effects not just upon its targets, but also on the prejudiced themselves. People who feel negative about aging live an average of 7.5 years fewer than people who have positive attitudes about aging."[12] Negative stereotypes (e.g., viewing the elderly as curmudgeons or severely impaired) can be replaced with more positive ones (e.g., viewing them as active older people and nurturing grandparents).

The three key dimensions for graceful aging are warmth, competence, and a sense of humor. Warmth encompasses both sociability and perceived morality or trustworthiness. One way to reduce prejudice against the aging is to increase contact with them, including intergenerational contact. One of the primary components of sociability and warmth is the presence of humor, which makes social situations more enjoyable, relieves anxiety, increases identification and social cohesiveness, and enhances the likability of a communicator.

Psychologist Rod Martin has categorized four different types of humor: self-effacing, life-affirming, bonding, and aggressive.[13] For young men, aggressive humor dominates; for older men, it takes an act of will to laugh with life-affirming joy.

The therapeutic benefits of laughter to health have been well documented. When we laugh, chemical endorphins are released into the bloodstream. As laughter provides a workout for the diaphragm, endorphins increase the body's ability to use oxygen. Laughter enhances blood flow, lowers blood pressure, stimulates alertness, dulls pain, fosters a sense of relaxation, provides cardiovascular benefits, increases levels of immunoglobulin in the natural immune system, and loosens bowels. Laughter truly may be good medicine, especially during that last process.

Heart disease has been identified as the number one killer among older men. Healthy hearts are helped by humor. A good laugh pumps the blood, but those who remain gloomy may find themselves in a cycle of sickness. A team of University of Maryland medical researchers found that people with heart disease were 40 percent less likely to laugh in humorous situations than those with healthy hearts.[14] Refusing to rejoice or be grateful in all situations has deleterious health effects, and deleterious health effects are not good at all. You might as well eat lots and lots of bacon at every meal.

One of laughter's most profound effects occurs within the immune system. Humor provides a safety valve that shuts off the flow of stress hormones, those fight-or-flight compounds that come into play during times of stress, hostility, and rage. People who are typically hostile and prone to anger are more likely to suffer heart attacks and sudden death than their chuckling, laid-back counterparts. The reason? Stress hormones, which include adrenaline, bombard the hearts of hostile (and anxious) people, forcing the organ to beat as if in a constant state of fight or flight.

In 2010, researchers from Wayne State University hypothesized that a big grin may help you live longer. The larger your smile, the more longevity you will enjoy.[15] Their study on "smile intensity" examined a large sample of headshot photographs from baseball players and categorized them according to "no smile," "partial smile," and the "full—or Duchenne—smile." They discovered that even a partial smile added years to one's lifespan, as those with no smile lived for 72.9 years, 2 years less than those with a partial smile. Players with full smiles lived to 79.9 years. Abel and Kruger's research complemented other studies, such as those that predicted socioeconomic status or that of Matthew Hertenstein, whose research on smile intensity in yearbook photographs could predict remarkably accurately whether the person pictured would go through a divorce.[16] The face reveals health.

At UCLA, studies on laughter demonstrated the reduction of pain in children undergoing painful medical procedures.[17] Remember the hospital face and pain charts: the better you feel, the bigger your smile. Researchers at the Loma Linda University School of Medicine measured the effects of laughter on stress hormone levels in groups of college students. After a humorous presentation, levels of stress were significantly reduced in the group that giggled. Brain activity changes when we catch the punch line of a joke. Endorphins go wild. (What is remarkable is that only 10–15 percent of laughter is at jokes. Most laughter stems from a sheer delight of living.[18])

Researchers also studied nursing home residents who participated in a humor therapy group and found that those who participated experienced "significant decreases in pain (physiological) and perceptions of loneliness and significant increases in happiness and life satisfaction (psychological)."[19]

There is a strong correlation between facial expression and emotional state. Psychologist Paul Ekman's research on emotional states and facial expressions demonstrates that emotions are connected to bodily behaviors: "We know that if you have an emotion, it shows on your face. Now we've shown it goes the other way too. . . . *You become what you put on your face*" (emphasis added).[20]

Such physiological insights confirm what the Scriptures observed centuries ago: "A happy heart makes the face cheerful" (Prov 15:13). But is the reverse true? Does a cheerful face help make a happy heart?

Evidence seems to say that it does. When we practice rejoicing and laughing, we find our spirits lifted.

Different muscles contribute to the authenticity and robustness of our laughter. The anatomical underwear of the polite smile is the *zygomaticus major* muscle, which connects the cheek bone with the corners of the mouth. This muscle creates the kind of voluntary smile one puts on to greet the minister after a service, with a "nice sermon, Pastor" with only the corners of the mouth lifting. It is the kind of smile one gives to an author when saying, "good book," thought one hasn't even peeked inside the cover. There are many *zygomaticus* moments in our lives.

However, when we feel genuine mirth, the fine sheath of *orbicularis oculi* muscles surrounding the eyes takes over. The squinting of these muscles signifies an authentic delight, so much so that the pupils dilate and a twinkle might appear. It will give us crow's feet (those fine wrinkles around the eyes), but it makes us feel like bluebirds.

The next two muscles concern the forehead and open the face. The *frontalis* muscle pulls the scalp back (if you are bald, it pulls it all the way to the back of your neck) so that the eyebrows are raised and the forehead can wrinkle. *Platysma*, which encompasses the collarbone up to the jaw, opens the face down. The lower lip and neck muscles pull down to show teeth. If you don't want anyone to bother you in the library, sit around with your *platysma* engaged. Babies, though, respond positively to such a toothy smile. Research has also indicated that the wider you smile, the longer you may live.[21] We may thus posit that despite his infirmities, Isaac smiled widely.

The abdominal and vocal muscles join in at this point, contracting our stomachs, expelling air, and moving us into hilarity. A Chinese proverb warns, "Beware the man whose belly does not move when he laughs." To stay young, it is essential to hear and feel laughter. It differs significantly from the mere smile, which does not move the body or interrupt breathing.

Finally, laughter grows through sundry kinetic movements into a communal stage as you start moving, rocking back and forth, slapping yourself, your knees, and even other people. You may lose control of your body, ending up in tears and, ultimately, exhaustion.

If you laugh while drinking milk, it might spill out of your nose. In 1972, in Denver, Colorado, I took a blind date to a party for a spaghetti dinner. I was funny. I was witty. I was laughing hard when a noodle came out of my nose. I didn't get a second date.

God has designed a close relationship between our bodies and our spirits, so there is a therapeutic benefit to rejoicing and rehearsing our laughter. One may surmise that the ideas people live by will lead to health or sickness.

The erstwhile father of existentialism, Søren "the kooky" Kierkegaard, wrote volumes on laughter. In his *Stages on Life's Way*, he noticed that most people dawdle in the aesthetic stage, the place where pleasure, fun, and beauty reside. It is a good place, but not the best.

The second stage is the ethical stage, where people recognize a moral obligation to others and a need for integrity in themselves. This is the point when many young people enter politics with the hope of making the world a better place.

Third, when people realize and confess that they are basically selfish, or sinful, when they see their folly and self-delusion, they fall into the religious stage. Here, for a Christian like Kierkegaard, is where people find a taste of the transcendent and of comedy. All of life is put in perspective, and it is a comic perspective. Kierkegaard said that when he was young, he found himself in the Trophonian Cave, the home of Zeus's oracle and a holy place that inspired such awe that people who visited it lost their ability to smile. Kierkegaard wrote that he saw people emerge terrified and pale and unable to laugh.

"But when I grew older," Kierkegaard continued, "and opened my eyes and contemplated the real world, I had to laugh and have not ceased laughing ever since."[22] Age does not need to kill our laughter.

C. S. Lewis agreed, acknowledging that among spiritual people, there has been a great deal of false reverence about spiritual matters.[23] We are flooded with too much solemnity and speaking in holy tones, in both religious and political discourse. "A sour religion is the devil's religion," wrote John Wesley (who was never that cheery himself, but at least his composer brother Charles wrote "come Thou long expected Jesus . . . joy of every longing heart").

This does not mean we must choose between being serious and comic. The opposite of serious is not comic but trivial. The opposite of comic is not serious but tragic. Thus, solemn teenage romantics like Shelley deplored the "withering and perverting spirit of comedy."[24] They preferred romantic tragedy. Not so the Christian. Our gigantic serious secret is joy. We must share it. As Mark Twain observed, the best way to cheer yourself up is to try to cheer up somebody else.[25]

Isaac, we believe, learned that for those who seek God, God will fill their mouths with laughter and their lips with shouts of joy. To echo his grandmother Sarah, "all who hear this will laugh with us." It is a remarkable apologetic of faith that we might offer laughter as well as our love to others.

Chesterton wrote that God hid one thing from us when God walked upon the earth: "He never concealed His tears; He showed them plain on His open face at any daily sight such as the far sight of His native city. Yet He concealed something. . . . There was some one thing that was too great for God to show us when He walked upon our earth; and I have sometimes fancied that it was His mirth."[26]

Anglican priest and registered nurse Elizabeth MacKinlay investigated the relationships among humor, laughter, spirituality, and aging in her book *The Spiritual Dimension of Ageing*. She found tremendous therapeutic value in the habits of humor and the practice of laughter among the elderly. One woman who feared she would die and her body wouldn't be found for days was able to transcend her fears by joking that perhaps her two cats would eat her.[27]

Even such gallows humor helps. One spinster put in her will that she didn't want any men for pallbearers: "they didn't take me out when I was alive," she said. "I don't want them taking me out when I'm dead."

MacKinlay found that images of God shape one's spiritual health and that individuals who can make light about getting old transcend the daily hassles of life. By accepting and laughing at the aging body, they avoid self-pity; they also do not deny, rationalize, or repress their problems.

For Isaac, the story is about falling apart and not being able to make wise and astute decisions at the end of life. Scams on the elderly proliferate, and Isaac was only the first to be hoodwinked. Today, Isaac would be duped by some online scoundrel stealing his money for a Florida land deal investment, threatening him with jail for an unknown, unpaid tax, or offering him millions from Nigeria.

What drained Isaac of much of his aged joy were his daughters-in-law, the daughters of the Hittites, women who allegedly spent their time in idolatry and adultery. One called Adah or Basemath (meaning "wearing jewelry or perfume") adorned herself with jewels and perfumed herself, dressed up for harlotry. Esau took his second wife, Judith, from Beeri the Hittite; she may have lived with Esau, but she "performed her needs elsewhere," if you know what we mean.[28] Rebekah didn't want any more kin like them, so she sent Jacob to take a wife from the house of Bethuel, her father's family.

To get back at his mother, Esau heard that she didn't want any daughters from Canaan and that his own wives displeased her, so he went to his uncle Ishmael and married two more outsiders, including Ishmael's daughter Mahalath, whose name, *ke-mehalah*, came to mean "affliction" for her in-laws.

Such is the reason that Rebekah had nagged her husband, saying, "I am tired of living because of the daughters of Heth; if Jacob takes a wife from the daughters of Heth, like these, from the daughters of the land, what good will my life be to me?" (Gen 27:46). And Isaac knew that if Rebekah wasn't happy, he would not be either.

It was a quiet ending for Isaac. After the family dysfunction, Jacob finally returned and was reconciled to his brother Esau. He met his father Isaac at Mamre of Hebron, whose days at this time were over 180 years. Then Isaac breathed his last and died and was gathered to his people, old and full of years. And his sons Esau and Jacob buried him.

We might hope that Isaac had lived out his name, that he who laughed best also laughed last. In *The Merchant of Venice*, Gratiano plays the fool and speaks to his sad friend Antonio, exhorting him, "with mirth and laughter let old wrinkles come" (Act I, sc. 1, line

83). The wrinkles of *orbicularis oculis* may prove genuine joy in old age.

Though we age, fall decrepit, and wrinkle, in a twinkling of an eye, in the sparkle that yet shows life, a loud trumpet will sound. The first to be raised from the dead and made new will be Isaac and his kin. No longer decaying, no longer delaying his laughter, Isaac shall be raised imperishable (2 Cor 15:52). His laughter shall resound throughout the heavens. The blind Isaac will see. The deaf Isaac will hear. The dead Isaac will be resurrected full of health and vitality, and he will be reunited with his old kin for a grand, and very large, family portrait. And everyone in the picture will be laughing as in Dutch painter Jan Steen's *The Merry Family* (1668). The note on the mantelpiece of the eating, drinking, laughing musical family reads, "As the old sing, so shall the young twitter." In other words, Isaac will have taught his children how to rejoice and laugh. The health of his laughter will have been passed down from one hearty generation to another, even to ours.

For Discussion and Further Reflection

1. When you think of Isaac, what stands out most about him? Is there anything not mentioned here?

2. Isaac's name literally means laughter. If your friend could choose a name for you that sums up your character, what might it be? Better yet, what trait do you hope they would recognize in you that is particularly meaningful for how you seek to live your life?

3. "Without a philosophy, or a theology, of change, a man stops in his tracks. Because most men are task oriented, they may not know what to do once the task is done. And many men do not discuss these things with other men. The male malaise is not shared. One goes at it alone." Are those statements fair? Can you think of examples from your own life?

4. Much of this chapter focuses on the body and the challenges it faces with age. Without giving an "organ recital," reflect on a physical aspect of aging that has caught you off-guard. Think about friends who struggle with various physical infirmities. How do they handle them with grace or with humor?

5. Laughter and humor can help us grow and be healthy. What are ways in which you experience laughter? What causes a belly laugh for you? How do you delight in living and playing?

Notes

1. You can listen to the sketch here: https://www.youtube.com/watch?v=RI7wDpBRqjo.

2. "Don v. Devil," *Time* (8 September 1947): 65.

3. Lewis Carroll, *Alice's Adventures in Wonderland* (New York: MacMillan Co., 1920) 63.

4. G. K. Chesterton, "Everlasting Man" in *Collected Works of G. K. Chesterton* (Book II) (San Francisco: Ignatius Press, 1987) 189. He adds "Both a baby and an old man walk with difficulty; but he who shall expect the old gentleman to lie on his back and kick joyfully instead, will be disappointed."

5. National Alliance on Mental Illness. Depression in Older Persons Fact Sheet, www.ncoa.org/wp-content/uploads/Depression_Older_Persons_Fact-Sheet_2009.pdf.

6. *As You Like It*, Act II, sc. 7, lines 26–27.

7. Jeremy Taylor, *The Rules and Exercises of Holy Dying* (Cambridge: E. P. Dutton & Co., 1876) 5–6.

8. Bryce A. Mander, Joseph R. Winer, and Matthew P. Walker, "Sleep and Human Aging," *Neuron* 94/1 (April 5, 2017): 19–36 (doi.org/10.1016/j.neuron.2017.02.004).

9. Gail Sheehy, *Understanding Men's Passages: Discovering the New Map of Men's Lives* (New York: Ballantine Books, 1999) 4.

10. Attributed to Leonard K. Hirschberg.

11. Mark Twain, *The Adventures of Tom Sawyer* (New York: Harper & Brothers, 1917) 244.

12. Chien-Yu Chen, et al., "Stereotype reduction through humor and accommodation during imagined communication with older adults," *Communication Monographs* 84 (2017): 94–109.

13. Rod A. Martin and Thomas Ford, *The Psychology of Humor: An Integrative Approach* (New York: Academic Press, 2018).

14. University of Maryland Medical Center, "Laughter Is Good for Your Heart, According to a New University of Maryland Medical Center Study," ScienceDaily. www.sciencedaily.com/releases/2000/11/001116080726.htm (accessed June 2, 2019).

15. Ernest L. Abel and Michael L. Kruger, "Smile Intensity in Photographs Predicts Longevity," *Psychological Science* 21/4 (April 1, 2010): 542–44.

16. Matthew Hertenstein, "Smile intensity in photographs predicts divorce later in life," *Motivation and Emotion* 33/2 (June 2009): 99–105.

17. Margaret Stuber et al., "Laughter, Humor and Pain Perception in Children: A Pilot Study," *Evidence-based Complementary and Alternative Medicine* 6/2 (June 2009): 271–76.

18. Seth Borenstein, "To Scientists, Laughter Is No Joke," http://www.nbcnews.com/id/36122340/ns/technology_and_science-science/t/scientists-laughter-no-joke/#.XQ0__S3MxTY (accessed June 21, 2019).

19. Brandon M. Savage, et al., "Humor, laughter, learning, and health! A brief review," *Advances in Physiology Education* , July 5, 2017, www.physiology.org/doi/full/10.1152/advan.00030.2017 (accessed June 3, 2019).

20. Ekman quoted in David G. Savage, "Expressions Trigger Emotions: Putting On a Happy Face: It Works, Researcher Says," *Los Angeles Times*, May 29, 1985, www.latimes.com/archives/la-xpm-1985-05-29-mn-7418-story.html (accessed June 3, 2019). See also Paul Ekman, *Unmasking the Face: A Guide to Recognizing Emotions from Facial Expressions* (San Francisco: Malor Books, 2003).

21. Shari Roan, "Life Span May Be as Long as Your Smile," *Los Angeles Times*, March 29, 2010, www.latimes.com/archives/la-xpm-2010-mar-29-la-he-capsule-20100329-story.html (accessed May 24, 2019).

22. Søren Kierkegaard, "Diapsalmata," www.ccel.org/k/kierkegaard/selections/diapsalmata.htm.

23. Sherwood Eliot Wirt, "Interview with C. S. Lewis," *Decision Magazine* (September 1963). Available at bensonian.files.wordpress.com/2012/04/interview.pdf.

24. As quoted by T. L. Peacock in "Memoirs of Percy Bysshe Shelley: Anecdotes of His Friends," *Frasier's Magazine* 57 (January–June 1858): 658.

25. As quoted in *The Wit and Wisdom of Mark Twain* (New York: Quarto Publishing Group, 2016) 116.

26. G. K. Chesterton, *Orthodoxy* (New York: John Lane Company, 1908) 298–99.

27. Elizabeth MacKinlay, *The Spiritual Dimension of Ageing*, 2nd ed. (Philadelphia: Jessica Kingsley Publishers, 2017) 303.

28. Tamar Kadari, "Esau, Wives of: Midrash and Aggadah," *Encyclopedia of Jewish Women*, Jewish Women's Archive, jwa.org/encyclopedia/article/esau-wives-of-midrash-and-aggadah.

Chapter 5

The Tricks of Jacob

Both as a young man and as an old man, Jacob lived an ironic life. As a young man, he duped others. As an old man, he was duped.

He first deceived his father, Isaac, and took advantage of his hungry brother, Esau. And that was the beginning of Jacob's mischief. God personally contended with Jacob. After Jacob wrestled with an angel or a "man," he discovered how God rules and engages God's people.

How does a Machiavellian trickster end up? Jacob, who cunningly caught hell from his elder twin, Esau, initiated what he feared to be a longstanding family feud. A mama's boy, he deceived his brother and his father for a birthright and a blessing. When it comes to inheritances, trusts, and wills, who knows if one can trust one's children or siblings?

But then, his mother, Rebekah, enabled him to escape with a blessing from Isaac. She complained about Esau's wives and nagged Isaac to send Jacob to a place where he could find some good women. When Esau heard that his mother and father didn't like his wives from Canaan, he went and got some more foreign women to add insult to injury.

What did Jacob do wrong? He was a bit ambitious, quite greedy, and very opportunistic. Taking advantage of his brother's appetites and his own father's frailties, he got ahead. He did well for himself. But success at the expense of another breeds distrust and fear—lots of fear.

Like his grandfather Abraham, Jacob was also a worrier, and for good reasons. When you cheat those closest to you, you wonder when the favor will be returned.

Remembering one's own sins, feeling not completely forgiven, makes it easier to remember the sins of others. Dorothy Parker quipped that "women and elephants never forget." So, it seems,

Jacob couldn't forget either. When one isn't trustworthy, it is hard to trust others. Jacob was the one who supplants, who had grabbed his brother's heel in the womb and erupted into the world riding on another's back. "I ain't heavy," he would sing. "I'm your brother."

The deeds we practice in youth can return to haunt us. We don't have to worry as much about the sins of the fathers being visited upon the sons as we do the sins of the sons being visited upon them when they become fathers. Like father, like son, yes, but even more, like the young man, so will the old man be (but probably worse).

When Jacob took off for Padan Aram to seek out his Uncle Laban, he wandered in the wilderness. Late one night, he lay down with a stone for a pillow and dreamed about a ladder (which, true to his nature of acquiring things, would become "Jacob's Ladder") reaching to heaven, with angels riding it up and down. And the Lord reiterated the promise given to Abraham and Isaac: "You and all the families of the earth shall be blessed."

When Jacob woke, he knew the Lord was in that place. And he got scared, righteously so. He realized how awesome the place was, even as the house of God and the gate of heaven. Taking his stone pillow, he set it on a pillar (a pillow pillar) and then sought to bargain with God.

Jacob didn't fully trust God. Jabez may have prayed a prayer of faith; Jacob haggled. Jacob's prayer sounds more human. Its formula is "Let's make a deal, God." Here are the conditions: "If God will be with me and keep me in this way that I am going, and give me bread to eat and clothing to put on, so that I come back to my father's house in peace, then the Lord shall be my God." The Lord had already promised all of this, but now Jacob wanted it in writing. The only thing missing was a galaxy of lawyers (or maybe a suit or gaggle of lawyers).

When Jacob got to the well (which would become Jacob's Well), he met the woman he wanted (just as Rebekah had come with the camels, now Rachel came with the sheep). He kissed her, and he cried.

Laban liked this nephew of his. He asked what his wages should be if Jacob worked for him. Jacob said he would work seven years for Rachel, but to anyone in love, seven years only seems like seven days.

Old Uncle Laban had the same genes as Jacob, but his hoodwinking skills were well practiced, and he could execute them with flair. First, because of the custom of marrying off one's firstborn, Laban gave Jacob the weak-eyed daughter, Leah, and not the babe, Rachel, for the wedding night. Jacob thought he was going to bed with Rachel, but he woke up with Leah. That happens a lot when guys pick up women at wells. We suspect that Laban plied Jacob with wine before the veil was lifted or lowered. The consolation prize? Laban required that Jacob bed Leah for only a week, and then he would get Rachel. The shifty Laban negotiated for another seven years of labor as well. Marrying sisters (and their respective handmaids) is not the wisest thing for a man to do, but Jacob stayed busy and soon had twelve sons.

Second, Laban tried to cheat Jacob with a contract for wages, giving him a flock of speckled and spotted sheep and goats and all the brown lambs. In a major application of an anachronism, Jacob was able to apply the selective breeding knowledge of nineteenth-century Augustinian friar Gregor Mendel, using dominant and recessive genetic engineering. He figured out how to cross-breed the animals to get the results he wanted. As such, the canny Jacob conned his father-in-law. The old trickster was tricked by the younger trickster. It wouldn't be the last time.

On the way to Canterbury, Chaucer's pilgrim the Reeve tells a similar tale of pranking. Two boastful students decide to fool a wily and crooked miller, who takes advantage of their inexperience, youth, and folly. Even though the students are fleeced of their grain, however, they then take advantage of the old man's schemes by bedding his wife and daughter.[1] The comic lesson shows all men to be fools. It is a democratic truth.

Jacob ended up with the choicest sheep and goats and took off for home in Canaan. He told his wives that their father's countenance was not too favorable to him, so it was probably a good time to leave. He told them Laban deceived him and changed his wages ten times, but God had protected and prospered him.

So Jacob fled with all his women and all his goods.

Now Jacob's greed infected his wife as well. Rachel, who didn't seem to know Jacob's God as well as he did, decided to bring along a few of Laban's gods. She sat on her camel on top of the household idols and pretended to be "in the manner of women," basically having her period so she couldn't move. Her clever ploy duped her father, and the clan escaped, even giving Laban a rebuke. But in the morning, Laban and Jacob and Rachel had waffles, probably cooked by Leah, and kissed each other good-bye with blessings all around.

Jacob was a con artist but still a fearful coward. Returning home to meet his brother, from whom he had absconded with his birthright and blessing twenty years earlier, a distressed Jacob divided his belongings and people into two companies. If Esau and his men attacked, the other company could escape. He also sought to appease his brother with generous bribes. Then Jacob put the women and children out front, in the more vulnerable company. He was afraid of what this older brother might do to him.

Fear strikes us all. I asked my students which they would fear more when they hadn't finished their final paper: seeing their professor coming down the hall or seeing a demon coming from hell. One-fourth of them confessed it would be the professor. The other three-fourths didn't see any difference.

Grace followed Jacob despite his fears. He got what he didn't deserve. Esau ran up to him and embraced him, somewhat like a preview of the prodigal son story.

Jacob had also taught his sons how to get along in the world—with a little deception and a little cunning. When their sister Dinah was raped by Shechem the Hivite, the boys devised a scheme for revenge. They promised a marriage with the Hivites if all the males would be circumcised. As soon as all the men were raw and vulnerable, Jacob's sons led in their massacre.

Then, after a life of savvy wheeling and dealing (and ending up on top), Jacob found himself old and duped by his own boys, who sold his pet son, Joseph, to the Egyptians. The trickster was tricked. "Your favorite son, Joseph," they lied, "was attacked by a wild beast. See, here is his pretty coat."

After losing Joseph, Jacob was overly cautious about Benjamin, his beloved Rachel's other son, whom she died delivering. Jacob kept Benjamin close. No fishing trips with the other brothers from other mothers. No trips to Egypt to secure food during the famine, lest some calamity befall him.

When Jacob was told that the Egyptian governor required that the brothers bring Benjamin back with them to retrieve Simeon and buy grain, he was beside himself. He lamented, "If anything should happen, you would bring down my gray hair with sorrow to the grave" (Gen 44:29).

Old age brings fears. Fears beget anxiety and murmuring. And murmuring begets sin, a lack of faith in the providence of God.

As the brothers went to Egypt for aid, Joseph finally revealed himself to them, acknowledging the sovereignty of God. "Don't be grieved or angry with yourselves because you sold me here," he said, "for God sent me before you to preserve for you a remnant on earth and to save your lives" (Gen 45:7).

Joseph sent his father ten donkeys loaded with the best things of Egypt and ten female donkeys loaded with grain and bread and all matter of sustenance. Even when such a gift horse came to Jacob, he was stunned and could not believe.

Finally, he sighed and said, "It is enough; my son, Joseph, is still alive and I will go see him before I die."

God had to remind Jacob again, in a dream, not to be afraid, for God was to make of him a great nation. Didn't his boys give him a tent full of children? Leah provided thirty-three sons and daughters, Rachel fourteen, Zilpah sixteen, and Bilhah seven (Judah's two naughty sons, Er and Onan, were not included, as they had died in Canaan). But such a family—seventy descendants in all! And Jacob's father only had two.

Even so, Jacob feared his end: "Ah, let me be carried down to Egypt where Joseph will close my eyes." When Joseph saw his father, however, he cried his eyes out and fell on his father's neck. He wept a long time, and one would think it would be of joy.

Appearing before Pharaoh as the patriarch of Joseph, Jacob was asked his age. "The years of my sojourning," he began ponderously, "are 130; few and unpleasant have been the years of my life; nor have they attained the years that my fathers lived" (Gen 47:9). Few and unpleasant. Not too many and not too good.

For Jacob, life has been nasty but too short. In other words, a few more nasty years would be welcome.

Yes, he had seen the Stairway to Heaven, and even hummed a few bars. But such days were in the past.

Jacob would live another 17 years to about age 147. He asked his son Joseph to place his hand under his thigh and promise to kindly and faithfully deliver him back to the graves of his fathers. In one sense, allowing your hand to be sat upon signifies submission. Decades earlier, Abraham's servant had enacted the same ritual with his oath to find a wife for Isaac. He would obey the master's command. He put himself under the rule of the father. It's like saying, "My hand is under your authority to do your good wishes." The odd symbolic gesture occurred when the patriarch was approaching death.

However, according to Rabbi Rashi from the *Midrash Rabbah* and Rabbi Tosefot in the *Talmud Shevuot 38b*, the thigh does not literally mean the thigh. What does it mean? Well, one must go a little higher. It means the *Milah*; it concerns the area of circumcision.

When you take an oath, or prepare to testify, you must hold in your hand a sacred object, such as a Bible, and promise to fulfill your office or tell the truth in court. What could be more sacred than a person's loins or holy testicles? Eliezer took Abraham's "thigh" and promised that his son Isaac would not have a wife from the daughters of Canaan; no forbidden relations for him. The circumcised must not fool around with the lustful uncircumcised.

If Abraham received a covenant for his "seed" to be passed on, the servant swore on the source of that seed, and the sign of the covenant was the painful reminder of circumcision. Swear on my testicles, which was pretty close to where the act of the Abrahamic covenant took place. The English word "testify" finds an etymological root in testicles. One testifies on one's testicles. Not that we would recommend such a testimony in court or church.

When Jacob received a promise from his beloved son Joseph, he bowed his head in worship. His name had been changed to Israel, but there was still a bit of old Jacob in him. He was sick, but he collected his strength to sit up in bed. He remembered how Rachel had died in the land of Canaan and he had buried her on the way to Ephrath (that is, Bethlehem). But he also remembered what God had promised and announced: that Ephraim and Manasseh would replace Reuben and Simeon. His eyes were as weak as his father Isaac's had been, but he embraced the boys and told Joseph that he had never expected to see his face again, and to see his children as well.

However, the eyes of Israel were so dim with age that when he blessed Joseph's two oldest sons, he mixed up the younger and the elder. Ephraim got the blessing over Manasseh. Oh well, there was precedent for it in Jacob's case. Nevertheless, Joseph was not pleased and tried to correct it, but his father stubbornly refused, reaffirming his own status—the younger brother shall be greater than the elder one.

Then Jacob called his sons for a reading of the will. When he gave them the Semitic blessing, he threw in a few curses with the prophecies.

Some, like Judah the lion, received good words with messianic implications (and the promise of wine and milk in abundance), and Zebulun got to dwell by the sea. Issachar, the strong donkey, liked rest a bit too much and would become a band of slaves. The ravenous wolf tribe of Benjamin would become "beloved of the Lord" (Deut 33:12) and bring forth two descendants named Saul, one a bad king and one a zealous Pharisee, the latter being transformed by grace into an apostle.

It is worth noting that Jacob's sense of humor spilled over when he got to talking about Gad, as he made puns on the name with words like troop (*gedud*) and tramp (*rud*). Such a wit, that Jacob.

But in his old age, Jacob did not forget grievances. He couldn't forgive. His firstborn and preeminent son, Reuben, had lain with his own concubine on his father's couch. Ouch. For this, Reuben lost his birthright. Judah would ascend, like most second sons in the Scriptures; Reuben would be consigned to being fickle, as unstable as water, due to his relationship with Bilhah, ending up as one of the lost ten tribes of Israel (although tangentially connected to the inventive Arnold Reuben, who from his New York City delicatessen would be remembered as a tasty sandwich, mixing in generous portions of corned beef, Swiss cheese, sauerkraut, and Russian dressing on grilled rye bread).

But a worse curse awaited the two wild, cruel, and angry sons, Simeon and Levi, who had planned the massacre at Shechem (Gen 34:25-31). Levi's descendants ultimately returned to serving as priests after the debacle with the golden calf (Num 8:18-19), but at this point, Dad did not deal too gently with these two brutes. Simeon's tribe, scattered about and marginalized, would be completely ignored.

When it came to his last days, Jacob asked the boys to bury him in the field of Ephram the Hittite, in the cave near Mamre in the land of Canaan ("remember, your great-grandfather bought it from the sons of Heth, and for a good price too"). Thus, Jacob finally went gently into that dark night, drawing up his feet into the bed and breathing his last, being gathered to his people. As was the Egyptian custom, he was embalmed and mourned for seventy days.

Possibly, Jacob trusted in his rest. His fear was wiped away. The gates of Sheol would not hold him forever, as they would be smashed and hell would be harrowed. The day death died would become known as Good Friday, a day of death that would forgive deceit. In the harrowing of hell, Christ himself descended into the dead and rescued those held captive. Such is a great, curious, and wonderfully strange part of the Christian creed. And one of those rescued would have been the trickster.

"Fear not," said Israel's Rescuer, "for I am with you." One of God's friends wrote that he was persuaded that "neither death, nor life, nor angels, nor principalities, nor things present, nor things to come, nor powers, nor height, nor depth, nor any other created thing, will be able to separate us from the love of God, which is in Christ Jesus our Lord" (Rom 8:38-39).

Jacob had been held captive by his own fears. Now he would be free, free at last. At the age of 150, Jacob died and was duped no more.

"Jacob, I loved," said the Lord. "Jacob, I loved." And it is that love that chases out fear.

For Discussion and Further Reflection

1. When you think of Jacob, what stands out most about him? Is there anything not mentioned here?

2. What stood out to you in this chapter?

3. Jacob was a trickster who was tricked. He deceived others, and even his father-in-law tricked him. Why is all of this deceit described in the Bible? Does it serve a broader purpose?

4. In Genesis 32, Jacob and his brother Esau are reunited after years of animosity and separation. Based on your experiences or your

observations, what situations create family division or division between friends or church members? What kinds of opportunities, situations, or initiatives can help people begin to overcome that division?

5. We all die. At Jacob's death, his sons surround him. If you were in that situation, what might you hope you would say—or be able to say—to the children, relatives, friends, or others who surround you?

Note

1. If your Chaucer is rusty, you can revisit the story—with modern translation—at sites.fas.harvard.edu/~chaucer/teachslf/rvt-par.htm.

Chapter 6

The Complaint of Moses

Mel Brooks, Val Kilmer, Soupy Sales, Ben Kingsley, Burt Lancaster, Charlton Heston, and Fraser Heston all have one thing in common: each played the main character in a movie about Moses. Fraser Heston and his father, Charlton, played Moses in the same film, *The Ten Commandments*. As a baby, Fraser Heston was in a basket in the Nile River, where he was found by the daughter of Pharaoh. He was sort of a method actor . . . as babies tend to be.

No figure is arguably more important to Judaism than Moses. And no biblical figure is more foundational to the story of the United States. The pilgrims quoted Moses' story, Washington and Lincoln were called his incarnations, and Ronald Reagan and Barack Obama cited him as inspiration. Bruce Feiler, author of *America's Prophet: How the Story of Moses Shaped America*, says it well: "Moses was more important to the Puritans, more meaningful to the Revolution, more impactful during the Civil War, and more inspiring to the immigrants' rights, civil rights, and women's rights movements of the last century than Jesus."[1]

One reason we might identify with Moses more easily than with Jesus is because he falls short of his goal. We can relate to him.

We first encounter Moses at the beginning of Exodus, when the Hebrew community in Egypt has become so large that Pharaoh is concerned. Even though these people had been in Egypt for some 500 years, almost half a millennium, Pharaoh realized that it was time to thin the herd. He treated them like animals and even used language that made them sound animal-like (for example, in Exodus 1:19, the women are described as "vigorous," which is a translation of the Hebrew word *hayyot*, related to the word for "animal"). He wanted them dead and even ordered Hebrew midwives to kill the newborn babies. Moses was supposed to have been drowned due to Pharaoh's declaration about killing all Hebrew babies, but the cunning Hebrew midwives, Shiphrah and Puah, defied the order and explained that the children survived because vigorous Hebrew women popped out the babies before the midwives could arrive.

When Moses was born, his mother took no chances. She hid him for three months and then put him in a papyrus basket in the Nile River.

The daughter of Pharaoh saw the basket, claimed it, opened it, and took the child as her own. Exodus 2:10 says she named him Moses because she "drew him out of the water." Moses means "drawn out" in Hebrew. As a baby, he was drawn out of the water. Maybe this Egyptian princess knew Hebrew and could predict the future. Maybe not.

What we do know is that the word "Moses" in Egyptian means "son," so perhaps the princess's name for this baby had two meanings, even one that she never fully intended. She called him "son," but he later drew the Hebrews from Egypt.

If we then look in the Bible for a story about the prince of Egypt or about antics of Moses growing up in the court of Pharaoh, we will be disappointed. Those stories are only in the minds of artists at DreamWorks Studios and Hollywood.

However, regardless of his origin, Moses' life began nobly. As described in Exodus 2, the first three stories of his life all focus on his concern with justice. First, he saw an Egyptian beating a Hebrew slave. Moses couldn't tolerate that, so he killed the Egyptian and buried him in the sand. It is difficult not to imagine a much older Moses on Mt. Sinai, holding two stone tablets with the Ten Commandments and looking sheepishly at the words, "Thou shall not kill." But that came later. Second, Moses tried to bring peace to two Hebrews who were fighting, until one of them said to him, "Who made you a ruler and judge over us? Do you mean to kill me as you killed the Egyptian?" (Exod 2:14). Moses then realized that he needed to leave, since Pharaoh would kill him once he discovered what he had done. So Moses escaped to Midian where—in the third story—he saved seven daughters from shepherds who had assaulted them and forced them away from a watering well.

Moses married one of these women, and soon he found a radically different lifestyle as he became a herdsman, watching his father-in-law's flock. In marrying Zipporah, Moses did gain a wise father-in-law named Jethro. The old man would later tell Moses that he was a workaholic and would not be able to keep it up. "Divide your labor," he told his son-in-law. "Appoint people you trust under you and let them make decisions and rulings. Build a system." Old age can offer wisdom. Gray hair has advantages. You learn to work wisely.

One day Moses encountered a life-transforming burning bush, a manifestation of God's presence. There God commanded Moses to go to Pharaoh. Referring to the enslaved Hebrews, Moses—as spokesman for God—was to tell Pharaoh, "Let my people go, so that they might serve me."

Moses did not want to do that, so he said, "I'm no one special." God responded. Then Moses offered another excuse, saying to God, "I don't know your name." God responded. Moses then said, "They won't believe me." God responded. Moses then said, "I am not eloquent." God responded. Finally, Moses said, "Send someone else." Each time God responded to Moses and gave him no way out except forward.

God's call to service was repeatedly met with Moses' reluctance and lack of enthusiasm. If Moses serves as a role model at this time in his life, it is largely for individuals like Samuel, Gideon, Isaiah, Jeremiah, Ezekiel, and Jonah—individuals who say "Who am I?" or "Send someone else" or "I'm too young." There is

a rabbinic tradition that says it took God seven days to persuade Moses. Six days to create the world, seven days to convince a man.

Moses said, "Who am I that I should go to Pharaoh?" God responded by saying, "I will be with you." God didn't say, "You can do it." God said, "I will be with you."

God called this 80-year-old man and Aaron, his 83-year-old brother, to go speak to Pharaoh. Speaking for God, they were to say to Pharaoh, "Let my people go." As we know, Pharaoh did not see it the same way God did. Pharaoh wanted to keep the Hebrews enslaved, so God sent Pharaoh clear signs that he should free the Hebrews. God sent ten plagues. The first was particularly appropriate: the Nile River turned to blood. In case we forgot how Pharaoh's persecution of the Hebrews started, it is helpful to remember that it began when Pharaoh demanded that the Egyptians drown the Hebrew babies in the Nile River. Years after that, the deaths in the Nile were remembered symbolically when the first plague involved the Nile River turning to blood. Then followed frogs, lice, flies, pestilence, boils, hail, locusts, darkness, and the deaths of firstborn children.

When Pharaoh finally let Moses and the Hebrews leave, the victory was short-lived, as the Hebrews soon were hunted down by Pharaoh's charioteers. When it seemed as if the charioteers would overcome the Hebrews, the Red Sea was parted, the Hebrews crossed on the dry land, and then, by the time the charioteers entered the seabed, the water came crashing back over them. The Egyptians were dead. The Hebrews were free.

A boy was sitting on a bench in a mall, reading and smiling. Talking to himself occasionally, he would say, "Hooray. Super." A man walking by asked the boy why he was so happy. The boy held his Bible and said, "Look what God is able to do. God opened the Red Sea and led the Hebrews through the middle to freedom." The man laughed, telling the boy, "That is explained easily. Scholarship shows that at the time, the Red Sea in that area was only 9 inches deep. The Hebrews just waded across." The boy was stunned. His eyes went from the man back to the Bible. The man walked on, but he had barely gone two steps when the boy said, "Hooray. Super." The man turned and saw the boy grinning. The boy said, "Amazing!

Not only did God lead the Hebrews through the Red Sea, but God also drowned the whole Egyptian army in 9 inches of water!"

The deaths that resulted were not simply forgotten, though. Within Judaism, one of the most beautiful of all rituals occurs during the Passover Seder, when the ten plagues are recited, and Jews remember each plague by dripping wine onto their plates until there are ten drops. Wine symbolizes joy, but those ten drops of wine are not to be drunk. That joy is gone. The drops of wine are a reminder of the suffering, not of the Jews but of the Egyptians. Dripping the wine is a reminder of the importance of empathy, of caring for others. It is one of the most gracious and other-focused religious acts of any religion. The exodus of the Jews from Egypt could not have happened without the deaths of the Egyptian firstborn and then the Egyptian deaths in the Red Sea. As a result, the joy is limited. As Proverbs 24:17 says, "Do not exult in the downfall of your enemies, and do not rejoice in their failure." The Egyptians were dead. The Hebrews were free.

God led the people out of Egypt, but that is not the end of the story. Time after time, God—through Moses—did not say to the Pharaoh simply "Let my people go," but said, "Let my people go, that they may serve me." And if the parting of the Red Sea ("let my people go") is the miracle most frequently associated with Moses, the freedom that it represents makes sense only when it is balanced with responsibility and meaning ("that they may serve me"), and that is represented most frequently by the incident that happened fifty days later, when Moses at Mt. Sinai received the Ten Commandments from God.

Humans blur boundaries and frequently dislike restrictions, but Moses presented the law of God as a sign of the love of God. It is meant for our good, no matter how restrictive it may appear at times. In 2006, Congressman Lynn Westmoreland of Georgia cosponsored a bill that would require the posting of the Ten Commandments in the U.S. Senate and House chambers. He also sponsored a bill that the Ten Commandments would be displayed in courthouses in a historical setting. In that year, in a segment for *The Daily Show*, Congressman Westmoreland was interviewed by Stephen Colbert on his comedy segment, "The Colbert Report." Colbert asked him why this bill was important. Westmoreland responded that if people didn't know the Ten Commandments, they could lose their entire moral grounding. Colbert then asked, "What are the Ten Commandments?" Westmoreland's eyebrows went up, and he responded, "What are *all* of them?" Colbert nodded his head. Westmoreland paused. Reflected. Looked into the distance. He then said, "Don't murder. Don't lie. Don't steal." Each time Westmoreland listed a commandment, Colbert raised a finger. Westmoreland listed only those three before he said, "I can't name them all." So only three fingers were raised. At the end of the interview, Stephen Colbert said to the congressman, "Thank you for taking time off from keeping the Sabbath day holy to be with us today." Apparently, the interview had taken place on the Sabbath. For those of us who champion the moral wisdom of the Ten Commandments, it would be wise to make sure we know them first. Then, we might try to obey them.

Without the Ten Commandments, humans could lose their moral grounding. The first of them focus on humans' relationship with God, while the latter focus on humans' relationship with each other. They create boundaries that, in turn, keep humans safe.

A priest and pastor from local churches are standing by the side of the road, pounding a sign into the ground that reads, "The end is near! Turn yourself around now before it's too late!" As a driver speeds by, he shouts out, "Leave us alone, you religious nuts!" From around the curve they hear screeching tires and a big splash. The pastor turns to the priest and asks, "Do you think the sign should have said 'Bridge Out'?"

Moses pointed to freedom through the exodus and to responsibility through the Ten Commandments. He brought together both parts of the commandment that God gave: "Let my people go" (freedom), "so that they may serve me" (responsibility).

Initially hesitant to follow God's command, Moses was won over by God. After bringing the Hebrews out of Egypt and sharing the Ten Commandments with them, Moses continued to lead them through the desert, en route to the promised land. In so many respects, Moses seems to be the ideal hero of the faith. But, in the book of Numbers, we are reminded that each of our lives is not over until the closing scene.

The Hebrew, or Jewish, title for the book of Numbers is translated "In the Wilderness," and that title describes well the contents of the entire book. The Hebrews are in the wilderness; they are lost, they are grumbling and discontent, they have eaten way too much manna, and Moses is doing his best to negotiate their complaints, but he is being worn down.

Constant complaining can do that. A man who wanted to become a monk went to the monastery and talked to the head monk. The head monk said, "You must take a vow of silence and can only say two words every three years." The man agreed, and after the first three years, the head monk came to him and said, "What are your two words?" "Food cold!" the man replied. Three more years went by and the head monk came to him and said, "What are your two words?" "Robe dirty!" the man said. Three more years went by and the head monk came to him and said, "What are your two words?" "I quit!" said the man. "Well," the head monk replied, "I am not surprised. You have done nothing but complain ever since you got here!"

Throughout the book of Numbers, Moses is riddled with complaints from those he is seeking to help. As old men, maybe we need to be particularly careful—in terms of our own character—when we face complainers. They can bring out the worst in us. And that is what happened to Moses. In Numbers 20, he responds to the Hebrews' complaints in a way that leads to his own downfall. For all of the ways Moses was faithful, his story ends short of the promised land, reminding us of the importance of finishing our earthly race strong.

In Numbers 20, the Hebrews arrive at Kadesh in the Desert of Zin. Their deep thirst causes them to bemoan both their lives and their having left the grain, figs, and water of Egypt. Moses goes to God, who says, "Take the staff, and assemble the congregation, you and your brother Aaron, and command the rock before their eyes to yield its water. Thus you shall bring water out of the rock for them; thus you shall provide drink for the congregation and their livestock"

(20:8). So Moses takes the staff, gathers the congregation in front of the rock, and says to them, "Listen, you rebels, must we bring you water out of this rock?" Moses then hits the rock twice with his staff, water flows out, and the community drinks.

God told Moses to take his staff and command the rock. But, for whatever reason, Moses referred to those gathered as rebels and said, "Must we bring you water out of this rock?" presumably pointing to his own ability to draw out water, implying that God could not do so. Moses did not command the rock, but instead he hit it twice. He expressed impatience, anger, and pride.

Until this point, every miracle that Moses did was through actions, but here he was to do a miracle through words alone. Maybe he wasn't ready to accept that God could do that. We all have limitations to the leaps of faith we are willing to take. There was a man fishing in Loch Ness one day when all of a sudden, he was tossed into the air. Not knowing what happened, he screamed, only to realize the Loch Ness monster was following quickly behind. Nessie had the man in her wide-open jaws, and right before she closed them, the man cried out, "Oh my God, help me!" And time stopped. The voice of God said, "Why should I save you? You've never believed in me a day in your life." To which the man replied, "Well, to be fair, up until this point I didn't believe in the Loch Ness monster either."

Although we don't know if Nessie ended up eating the man, we do know that Moses' actions had enduring consequences. After Moses hit the rock, God said to him, "Because you did not trust in me enough to honor me as holy in the sight of the Israelites, you will not bring this community into the land I give them."

The story of Moses continues throughout the book of Numbers and to the end of the book of Deuteronomy, where Moses dies on a mountaintop, looking across at the land that had been his destination.

Throughout the story of Moses, we see him grow from being riddled with self-doubt to taking on the Pharaoh, from crossing the Red Sea to receiving the Ten Commandments. Early in his life he had sold himself short, but in the Desert of Zin, the complaining perhaps became overwhelming to him, and so he exalted himself in ways that ignored who God was and what God had done. The story of Moses ends when he takes center stage, dramatically accuses the Hebrews, and hits a rock twice, as if he were engaging in miracles of his own doing.

"Let my people go, so that they might serve me" is the phrase that God repeatedly uses. Human freedom finds its meaning in service to God. God makes our name great—makes us a blessing—when we rely on the strength and power of God. But when we do not trust the promise of God, and when we begin to claim ourselves as being in charge, we will be humbled.

In the 1939 publication of his *Moses and Monotheism*, an unbelieving Sigmund Freud claimed that Moses was an Egyptian who invented it all and then was murdered in the desert. Freud had described Moses' belief in God as a collective neurosis in *The Future of an Illusion*, calling such faith a "longing for a father."[2] Yet, like most of Freud's hypotheses about projections of the psyche, this one goes both ways. One can believe that a Father in heaven is a mere projection of a human desire, or one can believe that there is no Father in heaven, which can also be a projection of a human desire.

Composed when he was suffering severely from cancer of the jaw, the 83-year-old psychoanalyst wrote his controversial work arguing that Moses was not Jewish. But such a flawed person had to be one of God's people. God hammered and chiseled him so that he would lead God's people to the promised land (they were God's people until they murmured and complained; then, God said they were Moses' people). And there at the end of his life, there on the mountaintop, because of one impetuous moment of being a crotchety old coot who lost his temper, Moses was refused entrance into the promised land.

This great Hebrew leader was an impatient man of God, and he was the first, since Adam, who knew God face to face (Deut 34:10). We suspect that kept him young. Yet, standing up on his vista on Mount Nebo to the top of Pisgah, he looked across at Jericho, a land filled with milk and honey, where giant clusters of grapes awaited God's children. God fulfilled the promise of giving this land to the people, letting Moses see it with his own eyes but not cross over to it.

Reflecting on Psalm 92:14, "bearing fruit even in old age," Rabbi Bradley Artson contrasted the natural aging of becoming full of sap and green with the artificial and futile ways that middle-aged women undergo cosmetic surgery, "bleaching hair, lifting faces, breasts, and calves, sucking off fat, and dressing in the gaudiest apparel possible" in an attempt to stay young forever.[3] Middle-aged men vainly try to ward off death, too, even buying sharp red convertibles or taking up vices like finding a young mistress or buying a toupee.

Rabbi Artson argues that one way to put off death is to honor the old, such as by spending time with Moses and Aaron. The Torah goes out of its way to show how old the two were (80 and 83, respectively) when they confronted Pharaoh. As Artson observes, "Not only do they not hide their age, but it is a source of pride." Eighty is the age of strength, of gathering wisdom from experience and completion. One has run the race and has finished well. Such a man can look at the human condition with "compassion and some skepticism. At 80 years of age, we need no longer serve either passion or ambition."[4] The Talmud views the elderly as healthy, according to Rabbi Hanina, "as long as one is able to stand on one foot and put on and take off one's shoes."[5] He remarked that "the warm bath and oil with which my parents anointed me in my youth have stood me in good stead in my old age."[6] The faith tradition is the warm bath, and the word of the Lord is the oil to anoint the old body and soul. "Then, even in old age, we will flourish like a cedar. Planted in the courtyards of our God, we shall bear fruit, even in old age."[7]

AARON, IT MAY BE THE PROMISED LAND FOR YOU BUT IT'S HEAVEN'S LAND FOR ME

Moses was planted on the top of Mount Nebo. Even though he was not permitted to enter the land of good and plenty, he could see the fruit of his calling. The book of Deuteronomy records that Moses was 120 years old when he died. "His eye was undimmed and his vigor unabated" (Deut 34:7). The phrase "may you live to 120" became a common blessing among the Jews. Moses had laid his hands upon Joshua, the son of Nun, who was filled with the spirit of wisdom, but the people remembered that "no one has ever shown the mighty power or performed the awesome deeds that Moses did in the sight of all Israel" (Deut 34:12). He is remembered, and that is good.

Being remembered well and envisioning his hopes, wedding the past and the future, Moses could rest. We are told that no one knows his burial place to this day, but the New Testament book of Jude tells the story of how the devil argued with Michael the archangel over Moses' body. It seems the accuser wasn't content to leave the old hero alone, even to remind him he hadn't gotten into Canaan, but God let old Moses rest (Jude 1:9).

Moses could rest, at least until the Transfiguration, when he and old Elijah appeared with Jesus, bringing the Law and Prophets together in one glorious moment. We can be sure of one thing: His face was shining again.

We should add a postscript about Joshua. The Bible tells us that "Now Joshua was old and advanced in years; and the Lord said to him, 'You are old and advanced in years, and very much of the land still remains to be possessed. . . '" (Joshua 13:1). My rector, Father Andy Buchanan, reflected on this passage and wrote, "Think of how people approach aging in our culture . . . . You run into someone you haven't seen for a while and they say, 'You look really good . . . for your age.' That's not how the Lord handles it with Joshua—he's so direct: Joshua, you're old. Our culture worships youth, strains to stay youthful. We all know you get older, but we resist it. . . ."

But the Hebrew perspective is this: "The longer you live, the more you can see about how God works. And the more you understand how He works, the more you can encourage those young whippersnappers. And the good news is that God is never finished with us when life and circumstances change. You know in the ancient world there was no retirement—we never reach the point where God wants us to do nothing. While we're here God always has something for us to do." In this biblical view of old age, one is not invited to retire, but to continue to serve. Even if it is just to say, "that's not how we did it in our day."

For Discussion and Further Reflection

1. When you think of Moses, what stands out most about him? Is there anything not mentioned here?

2. What stood out to you in this chapter?

3. It took a long time for Moses to be convinced to answer God's call. That is fairly typical, in part because we can be blind to God's call or not acknowledge it. Have you experienced God's call in your life? If not, why? Do you think you have experienced it and, like Moses, ignored it?

4. The Ten Commandments are presented in both Exodus 20 and Deuteronomy 5. The first of them focus more on relations with God, while the latter focus on human relations. Look at each of the Ten Commandments. Which matter least to people today (i.e., which are readily and easily broken)? Which do you find challenging?

5. Complainers can bring out the worst in us, much as they did with Moses. When do complainers frustrate, irritate, or anger you? Is it under certain circumstances or during specific times? What techniques do you have for responding in a godly manner to those who push your buttons? When do you find yourself complaining? Reflect on how you might express yourself differently.

Notes

1. Bruce Feiler, *America's Prophet* (New York: William Morrow, 2009).

2. Sigmund Freud, *The Future of an Illusion*, trans. and ed. James Strachey (New York: W. W. Norton & Co., 1961) 28.

3. Bradley Artson, "Bearing Fruit Even in Old Age," *My Jewish Learning*, www.myjewishlearning.com/article/bearing-fruit-even-in-old-age/.

4. Ibid.

5. Ibid.

6. Hanina, quoted in ibid.

7. Ibid.

Chapter 7

The Carnality of David

There is no greater beginning to leadership than God's appointment of David to be king of Israel. The book of Acts records that "After removing Saul, God made David their king. He testified concerning him: 'I have found David son of Jesse a man after my own heart; he will do everything I want him to do'" (Acts 13:22).

If there were a biblical figure who would seem to rise above the rest, it would be the young shepherd boy David who became Israel's greatest king and God's beloved servant. His later years were marked by vindictiveness and bad habits that he passed on to an allegedly wise son. A mean streak appeared.

Putting King David in this category of old men not getting better seems problematic. After all, he was a man after God's own heart. Humble, reverent, loving, diligent, devoted, faithful, a leader among men. He was considered so pious that anything he asked from God would be given. He was a poet, a warrior, a musician, a true leader, a gracious enemy, a devoted friend, and, er, a great lover of women. Who could ask for anything more?

Well, a friend and colleague, Rabbi Michael Panitz, provided a clue as to why David might be included in our list. He pointed out that when the books of history (Samuel and Kings) were assembled in Babylon, the scribes had been wondering, "What good did having kings do us? Even the best of them fell short of God's governance."

Such a thought goes back to two episodes: the first with King Abimelech, whose name means "my father was king" (which he wasn't, but who's to challenge a man in power?), and the second with the people clamoring for a king.

In the first, a parable of trees and brambles warns Israel about having a king; in the second, God himself concedes to their stubborn persistence to be like other nations.

In the book of Judges, when the trees wanted a king, they approached the fig tree, the olive tree, and the vine to see if any of them would fill the role. "No," they all responded, "we are too busy being productive. We feed people and make them glad. Figs, olives, and wine make men merry. What good can we do in government?" So the trees went to the brambles, who gladly became politicians and made brambles out of the nation (Judg 9:7-15). You want someone other than God to lead you? Well, here you go. You deserve the leaders you get.

Thus, God will show that no king could reign over the people better than the King of kings. "You think these are good leaders?" God asked. "Let me show you something about them. Even David and Josiah, the cream of the crop, did not wear well as they aged."

Noticeably, David (and subsequently his son Solomon) had problems with lust. Like father, like son. In the old days, the son would take on the sins of the father. As Solomon grew old, his wives turned his heart after other gods, and his heart was not fully devoted to the LORD his God, as the heart of David his father had been. These two men preceded Lord Byron by centuries, but they exemplify the poet's words well: "Let us have wine and women, mirth and laughter, / Sermons and soda water the day after."

An old, rusty poem often attributed to James Ball Naylor captures that sentiment as well, pointing back to the days of the Hebrew's merry monarchs:

King David and King Solomon
Led merry, merry lives,
With many, many lady friends
And many, many wives.
But when old age crept over them —
With many, many qualms! —
King Solomon wrote the Proverbs
And King David wrote the Psalms.

The "naughty" lives (as Monty Python would put it, "nudge, nudge, wink, wink, know what I mean?") of these two circumcised Casanovas would lead to plenty of leisure where they found balm for their troubled consciences by writing psalms and proverbs. Qualms about their immoral behavior would lead to much devotional and wisdom literature. But many of these escapades were in their youth. Later in life, they could only look back and reflect on them. Sometimes with guilt.

David was still one of the most remarkable and extraordinary men of God, reigning from about 1010 to 970 BC. He married, at first, out of political expediency. King Saul "gave" him his second daughter, Michal, as a snare to trap David. First, David had to gather 300 foreskins as a dowry (which were not included in any hope chest as far as we know), and second, he married this woman who would eventually find his dancing before the ark to be common and foolish.

He also gathered seven other wives over time: Ahinoam the Jezreelite, seemingly a political choice; the brilliant Abigail the Carmelite, formerly married to Nabal, the biggest dunce in the book of Kings; Maachah; Haggith; Abital; Eglah; and then finally Bathsheba. And this doesn't even begin to include his concubines.

By the time his tree should be withered, David serves as a model for Shakespeare's Adam, who confesses of himself in *As You Like It*, "Though I look old, yet I am strong and lusty [healthy, in this context]" (Act II, sc. 3, line 48).

In battle, he was savvy and courageous. He conquered Philistines, Moabites, Ammonites, Edomites, and every other kind of mite one could find in the neighborhood.

In meeting with adversaries, he was gracious (sure, the beautiful Abigail came to plead for her idiotic husband and became a wife) and long-suffering. The unrestrained gadfly Shimei incessantly swore at David and threw stones as the king fled Jerusalem. But David reflected, "If he curses and if the Lord has told him, 'Curse David,' then who shall say, 'Why have you done so?'" (2 Sam 16:10).

His son Absalom sought to usurp the kingdom and sleep with his father's concubines in the center of the city, yet David was heartbroken when his son got caught in a tree due to his long hair and was put to death by the ruthless general Joab. Absalom's death was a fulfillment of Nathan's prophecy that the sword would never depart from David's house. David would cry out, "O my son, Absalom, my son, my son Absalom! Would I have died instead of you, O Absalom, my son, my son." Such a lament would be echoed when William Faulkner used a Southern accent to revive it in his 1936 novel *Absolom, Absolom!*

As David returned to the Jerusalem, he met an old Gileadite named Barzillai, who had once been a great man and a supporter of the king. David invited him to cross over the Jordan with him, but Barzillai demurred: "What? I am now eighty years old. Can I distinguish between good and bad? Or can your servant taste what I eat or what I drink? Or can I hear any more the voice of singing men and women? Why then should your servant be an added burden to my lord the king?" (2 Sam 19:31-39). He begged to be allowed to stay in his own city and die. Recognizing the advent of age, David kissed the old codger and blessed him.

As David grew old, he had to stop fighting. Delivered from all his enemies, he composed a song to the Lord, his rock and his fortress. He remembered how God had rescued him in his distress, how the Lord delighted in him in his day of calamity.

The Lord had created in him a new heart, and David had kept himself from iniquity. His psalm declared that with the kind, God showed himself kind; with the pure, God was pure; and "to the devious you show yourself shrewd" (2 Sam 22:27). For David, it was time to be astute. He would pursue his enemies and destroy them and not turn back until they were consumed, devoured, shattered, and pulverized as the dust of the earth. In his last song, David celebrated his mighty men—men of valor, strength, and courage. They all killed many quite well and quite decisively.

In spite of his military prowess and spiritual inspiration, David made some faulty decisions in his last days. Against the advice of Joab, he commanded that the people be numbered. But David repented and asked the Lord to forgive his foolishness. Nevertheless, he was confronted with three consequences: seven years of famine, three months of being pursued by enemies, or three days of pestilence. He chose the last, a plague, and a great number of men died. David pleaded that it was he who sinned and entreated for his sheep, asking that the hand of the Lord be against his house only (2 Sam 24: 11-17).

The next years were not too promising. It may be that David developed dementia because he remembered only early slights against himself. As one old sage recognized, David in his psalms always repented, praised God, thanked God, and sought forgiveness from God, but he didn't seem to forgive others. This small shortcoming, another Baobab weed, would fester into something toxic. He had tasted the mercies of God, but he didn't practice the grace of God.

Dementia causes similar symptoms. People are less likely to show compassion to others. They are more likely to remember painful episodes in life. They hold on to grudges and speak more profanely, angrily, and what we might even call uncharacteristically. The seeds that are buried early in life begin to flower when old people no longer have the filters to hold back who they are: people in need of grace.

The first line of 1 Kings tells us, "King David was old, advanced in age; and they covered him with clothes and he could not keep warm." Old men get cold, especially their feet. But David's servants found him a beautiful girl named Abishag the Shunammite and put her in bed with him; still, he could "gat no heat" (1 Kings 1:1-4). Old age is really, really sad. Nevertheless, Abishag ministered to him, even when Bathsheba came to see him (1 Kings 1: 15-21). But Bathsheba had other concerns on her mind.

David's sons had continued to bring him grief. His fourth son and seemingly natural heir, the handsome Adonijah, claimed the throne when David crept toward his end. With the help of the prophet Nathan, Bathsheba reminded David that he promised that Solomon would succeed him.

A presumptuous Adonijah assumed he would be crowned. He sat eating and drinking with his buddies, like Joab, everyone cheering, "Long live King Adonijah!" But David placed Solomon on the throne instead, having him anointed by Zadok the priest and Nathan the prophet, with the trumpet celebrating his coronation. With flutes and cheers and great noise and rejoicing, Solomon rode the donkey to acclaim.

Realizing his predicament, a terrified Adonijah (who had gamely tried to usurp the throne) ran to the altar and took hold of the horns for his own safety, entreating Solomon not to put him to death (1 Kings 1:50). This scene turned out well . . . at least for a short while.

Bedridden and feeble, David prepared to meet his Maker. But his last thoughts and words didn't look forward to glory. He did counsel Solomon to walk in the ways of the Lord, but what isn't caught can't be taught. Solomon would inherit wisdom, but not for his personal life.

David's penultimate words, however, were about revenge. Like some Italian godfather, a Don Corleone of Israel, he instructed Solomon about getting an eye for an eye. The story doesn't gloss over anything. In his lifetime, David had been quite magnanimous, but now, old and ready to die, he wanted a few balance sheets corrected. He directed Solomon to repay in kind people who had aided him and those who had wronged him. He muttered that every one of the worthless should be thrust away like thorns.

"I am going the way of all the earth," he told his son (1 Kings 2:2). One expects great words to fall from the lips of the dying. At first, David doesn't disappoint: "If your sons are careful of their way, walking before God in truth with all their heart and all their soul, you shall not lack a man on the throne of Israel." Alas, with Solomon's two divisive sons, this wouldn't happen.

Then David whispered in a somewhat gravelly voice,

And you know what Joab did to me [he listed a litany of griev-
ances] . . . . So act according to your wisdom and do not let his
gray hair go down to Sheol in peace. But to that old Barzillai, older
than me, let him eat at your table. But then, that old son of Gera
the Benjamite, Shimei, remember he violently cursed me and I
promised not to put him to the death with the sword. Well, you
didn't promise that; therefore, do not let him go unpunished, for
you are a wise man and you will know what you ought to do to
him, and you will bring his gray hair down to Sheol with blood. (1
Kings 2:5-9)

"Take their gray hairs down to Sheol." After these last sharp
words, David slept with his fathers and was buried in the city of
David.

Solomon kept his
promises to his father. Even
Adonijah was safe until he
overstepped his bounds and
asked for the comely maid
in David's bed, Abishag
the Shunammite. Solomon
realized the conspiracy in
the bones of his brother
and had him killed. Joab
grabbed the horns of the
altar as well, seeking sanctuary, but to no avail. As
long as Shimei stayed in
his sanctuary city, he would
be fine, but he wandered.
Benaiah, Solomon's chief
henchman, fell upon them
all.

In his history in the book of Acts, Luke records that "for when
David had served God's purpose in his own generation, he fell asleep.
His body was buried with his fathers and saw decay" (13:36). David's
body was buried, and it saw decay.

The vices of old King David are mostly forgotten in the repeated tales of his battle with Goliath, his lyre playing for Saul, his friendship with Jonathan, and the love of his people. But his body decayed. Here is a sign of need and of hope.

Corruptible bodies not only decay; they stink.

Yet David knew the power of fragrance. One gets a sense of the value of aromatics in the Bible, of what we might call the "common scents" of the word of God.

In giving Moses instructions for incense in the tabernacle, the Lord ordered the finest of spices, such exotic resins of stacte, onycha, galbanum, pure (and the most aromatic) frankincense, flowing myrrh, cinnamon, fragrant cane, cassia, and a whole hin of olive oil. Out of all these sweet spices, the Lord told Moses, "You shall make of it the Anointing Oil, a fragrant mix, the work of a perfumer" (Exod 30:25). As such, it became a sacrament for the nose, the outer and visible sign of an inward and spiritual grace.

The word "anoint" connects us to the Latin *inunctus*, which literally means to smear with oil, to sanctify and consecrate. The word "Messiah" (and its Greek counterpart *Christos*) suggests the process of being anointed with holy oil. When Mary took a pound of costly perfume, she anointed the feet of Jesus and wiped them with her hair, and "the house was filled with the fragrance of the perfume." And on the third day of Jesus' death, Mary Magdalene, Mary the mother of James, and Salome brought spices to anoint what they thought would be the stinking body (even after Nicodemus had prepared him with a mixture of myrrh and aloes before wrapping him in linens) (Mark 16:1).

In one of the royal psalms, garments fragrant with myrrh and aloes and cassia are celebrated. (So, too, Solomon in all his wisdom would advise sprinkling one's bed with myrrh, aloes, and cinnamon in Proverbs 7:17.)

One marketer has patented an authentic cologne from the Holy Land named King David Biblical Perfume, Eau de Toilette for men, straight from Ein Gedi in Israel. With base notes of cedar, sandalwood, amber, and musk, as well as top notes of fig leaf, mandarin orange, cardamom, tarragon, lemon, and lavender, one suspects that the wearer would always smell good. What a divinely human fragrance for old men. But it will not keep one from stinking when the body decays.

Old men smell. Our feet, our breath, our unending happy flatulence (better than the stench of rotten eggs and the burning sulphur of Hades or the excess of Bay Rum cologne that some old men overuse).

It's like the old man sitting in the bar muttering over his beer. A stranger asks, "What's the matter?"

He replies, "I was a great professor for forty years. My teaching was electrifying and my students achieved great things, but do they call me Fraser the Professor? *No.*

"I was a renowned global scholar whose books sold in the millions, and my lectures appeared on YouTube, but do they call me Fraser the Scholar? *No.*

"I was an ambassador to nations, bringing goodwill among many countries and building reconciliation, but do they call me Fraser the Humanitarian? *No.*"

He paused, then said, "But I fart once in public and . . . ."

Yet, in spite of this natural stench we carry, this smudge of sinful humanity that soils our very presence, God makes us pleasing to his nostrils. Through Christ, God manifests the sweet aroma of the knowledge of him everywhere. "For we are," wrote the stinky apostle Paul, "a fragrance of Christ to God among those who are being saved and among those who are perishing: to the one an aroma from death to death; to the other an aroma from life to life. And who is adequate for these things?" (2 Cor 2:15).

If David wasn't adequate, and Paul wasn't adequate, how could we be adequate? Nevertheless, Christ loved us and became a sacrifice to God as a fragrant aroma for us. He cleaned and freshened us up.

My friend and co-author, Craig, studied in Germany with a distinguished professor who opined that the disciples got lost and couldn't find Jesus' tomb. When they finally got there, Jesus' body had decomposed and so it was never found; it was only assumed to have been raised. Craig shook his head back and forth when the professor said this, stunned that such an incredible fiction could be invented. But after he told a friend, she laughed, and every year on

Easter she would call him and—laughing uproariously—would say, "He has decomposed. He has decomposed indeed!" The parody of the genuine proclamation compels one to believe even more in the resurrection.

In preaching about the resurrection at Pentecost, the apostle Peter proclaimed that Christ's body saw no corruption (Acts 13:37). He has no tomb to mark his memorial. Remembrance of him comes in the breaking of bread and blessing of wine. Like the two disciples who walked to Emmaus, when one sits with Jesus, even incognito, one finds one's heart burning with joy and life.

David's body suffered decay, but there was one greater than David who came. And he promised to David and all those who follow him that he would give new life and an incorruptible body. It is the greatest hope of all. Jesus became a fragrance for men that was sure to last forever—and one that might also attract some older women in the meantime.

He is not decomposed. Christ is risen. He is risen indeed.

For Discussion and Further Reflection

1. When you think of David, what stands out most about him? Is there anything not mentioned here?

2. What stood out to you in this chapter?

3. Take some time to read the story of David and Bathsheba in light of the seven deadly sins (pride, anger, lust, greed, gluttony, avarice, and sloth). In this story, each sin is committed. Note each one. Make observations about how this story can shape our understanding of sin.

4. In our old age, particularly in dementia, words come out of our mouths that we—at earlier times—would have hoped to keep covered. Do you have any fears of what might come out of your mouth in the future? Do you feel the need to try to get some things straight in your life while you still can?

Chapter 8

The Folly of Solomon

Solomon was known for being the son of King David. He was known for building the temple and palace complex in Jerusalem. He is known today for having written more than 2,000 proverbs. Stories have been told of his famed wisdom and the wise ways in which he negotiated between disputants. But as an old man of the Bible, he casts a dark shadow over many of his accomplishments. Puffed up by attention from foreign women like the Queen of Sheba, his wisdom too easily slipped into folly. By looking at his life through two writings attributed to him—the Song of Songs and the book of Ecclesiastes—we see both the seeds of his problems as well as their fruit.

Solomon's growing addiction was hoarding women, hundreds of them, some on shelves, some in beds, some possibly as footstools. We are told that he "committed all the sins his father had done before him; his heart was not fully devoted to the LORD his God, as the heart of David his forefather had been" (1 Kings 15:3).

When discussing the 700 wives and 300 concubines of Solomon, the King James Version of the Bible, published in 1611, translates 1 Kings 11:1 as "King

Solomon loved many strange women." Modern versions translate the word "strange" in this verse as "foreign," but, with 700 wives and 300 concubines, at least some of them were probably strange. At the very least, one strange relationship is presented in the Song of Songs.

At times steamy and sultry, this song consists of shared words exchanged between two lovers. In 7:2-3, the man says to his beloved, "Your navel is a rounded bowl that never lacks mixed wine. Your belly is a heap of wheat, encircled with lilies." Women today might respond by saying, "What? My navel is like a punch bowl? What are you trying to say?"

The metaphors are foreign to us. The male character in the Song of Solomon describes his lover by whispering, "Your eyes are doves behind your veil. Your hair is like a flock of goats, moving down the slopes of Gilead. Your teeth are like a flock of shorn sheep" (4:1b-2). When he also compares his lover's forehead to a slice of pomegranate (4:3b; 6:7), we can see that his metaphors don't translate well. Two thousand years from now, our terms of endearment might sound equally strange: words like honeybun, pumpkin, and sweetheart may sound much more edible and foreign than they do to us today.

Aside from the metaphors, what might raise questions for us is that the word "God" is not mentioned in this entire book. There also is no theology or moral lesson. The man and woman do not seem to be married; thus, their romance seems forbidden and not all that restrained. Around 2,000 years ago, Rabbi Akiba acknowledged this by noting that some irreverent young people had been singing it in ancient taverns and bars (Tosephta Sanhedrin 12.10). He specifically commanded people not to sing it as a drinking song.

Our inhibitions frequently make it challenging to talk about sexuality. A little boy asked his mother where he came from and also where she had come from as a baby. His mother told him a story about a beautiful white-feathered bird, a stork. The boy asked his grandmother the same question, and she told him about the birds and the bees. Afterwards he said to his friend, "You know, there hasn't been a normal birth in our family for three generations."

Sometimes parents find it easier to hide behind a stork or the birds and bees than to speak openly about sexuality. That is one reason that the Song of Solomon is so remarkable. Solomon is said to have composed 1,005 songs (1 Kings 4:32) and had almost as many lovers. He had 700 wives and 300 concubines (1 Kings 11:3), so some kind of writing about love seems appropriate for him. However, if we think of sex in monogamous terms, we might see Solomon—with his many wives—as unfaithful or lascivious, not to mention exhausted.

Many of these marriages likely were not romantic in any sense; they were born from political alliances, with the marriages serving to discourage wars between different kingdoms. Although these marriages did not necessarily lead to sexual infidelity, they did lead to infidelity to God.

These relationships led Solomon to "turn away his heart after other gods; and his heart was not wholly true to the LORD his God, as was the heart of David, his father" (1 Kings 11:4). Solomon went after Ashtoreth, Micom, and all sorts of other goddesses. He built an altar for Chemosh and for Molech. He created temples for foreign gods and helped his wives offer sacrifices and burn incense to their gods. Solomon was so focused on building his legacy that he overlooked the ways that legacy led him away from God. It isn't surprising, only sad, that there is no mention of God in the Song of Solomon. What we do see in this writing is the kind of single-minded devotion that comes to be seen as the relationship each person of faith should have to God, and to God alone.

The book of 1 Kings celebrates Solomon as a pious, wise, and just ruler with the Queen of Sheba broadcasting his success. He has huge treasures of gold and even his wives seem happy (10:7), which is a miracle in itself. The annual weight of gold that Solomon accrued annually was 666 talents (not an auspicious sign for apocalyptically minded students). Silver was cheap, so he fashioned everything with gold, and every three years his ships brought him new gold, ivory, apes, and baboons. He looked blessed to any casual observer.

However, a study of Deuteronomy 17:14-20, which sets out criteria for a good king, challenges that royal portrait. Against those criteria, Solomon looks more like a king who violated at least half of the regulations of the covenant. He almost makes Jerusalem into a second Egypt. Both empires had massive building projects, and both forced immigrants (Hebrews and Canaanites) to make bricks and do heavy labor. Both acquired vast armies of chariots and horses, and when Israel was warned not to turn back toward Egypt, Solomon negotiated with Israel for his military and also married a daughter of Pharaoh. The writer of Deuteronomy sets up a plumb line that shows that this wise and wealthy king of Israel may have been no better than a pharaoh.

He looks wise, wealthy, and successful. But in his later years, one notices a loss of faith and a world-weariness. The rabbis said Solomon wrote the book of Ecclesiastes in his old age.

In the opening line of Ecclesiastes, he reflects on life and writes, "Vanity of vanities! All is vanity!" (1:2). The exact Hebrew words are translated into English in a variety of other ways as well: "Meaningless of meaningless! All is meaningless!" "Futility of futilities, all is futile!" "Utterly senseless. Utterly senseless, everything is senseless!"

Ecclesiastes is said to have been written by this son of David, this king, who had fully experienced wealth, knowledge, entertainment, food and drink, and then realized that it was all nothing. He writes how he had constructed great works, houses, and vineyards, and how he had slaves, silver, gold, entertainment, and everything imaginable. But none of that satisfied him, so he turned to wisdom, pleasure, laughter, and wine, and then he finally recognized that "all was vanity and a chasing after wind, and there was nothing to be gained under the sun" (1:11).

In Ecclesiastes, again and again, that is the refrain: there is nothing new under the sun; there is nothing to be gained under the sun. King Solomon offers a sincere reflection about how he tried to find meaning in his possessions, laughter, entertainment, wisdom, and even wine, but nothing satisfied. None of it helped. And the first time we listen to these words of Solomon, we may think we know what he is doing. He seems to be preparing to point to God, where ultimate meaning is found.

But he does not do so. He goes on to say that we can't really know God's will (3:10-11). Furthermore, he insists that good and evil people face the same fate (9:2-4): "the race is not to the swift, nor the battle to the strong, nor bread to the wise, nor riches to the intelligent, nor favor to the men of skill; but time and chance happen to them all" (9:11).

What is most striking about these words is the total lack of interest in faith. These are the words of someone who is not only world weary but also has come to lack a moral or spiritual compass. Nothing matters. In 3:2, he seems to shrug his shoulders and say, "There is nothing better for a man than that he should eat and drink, and find enjoyment in his toil."

At the end of the book, in what seems to be a later addition from an editor, these two verses appear: "The end of the matter; all has been heard. Fear God, and keep his commandments; for this is the whole duty of man. For God will bring every deed into judgment, with every secret thing, whether good or evil" (12:13-14).

Those verses don't fit with the rest of the book, and the rest of the book is so relentlessly pessimistic that it is no surprise that many rabbis opposed the whole thing. Any meaning to life seems elusive in this book, and the sentiment of the last two verses seems somewhat contrived.

Thomas Cathcart tells the story of a seeker who hears that the world's wisest guru is living at the top of India's highest mountain. The seeker travels far to get there, and then he climbs the steep mountain, in the process repeatedly stumbling, slipping, and falling. When he reaches the top, he is covered in cuts and bruises but grateful to see the guru, sitting cross-legged in front of a cave. The seeker says,

"O, wise guru, I have come to ask you what the secret of life is." "Ah, yes, the secret of life," the guru says. "The secret of life is a teacup." The seeker responds, "A teacup? I came all the way up here to find the meaning of life and you tell me it's a teacup?" The guru shrugs, and responds, "So maybe it isn't a teacup."[1]

Like the guru's response, the answer given by Solomon's words, or, for that matter, by the editor's addition, is unsatisfying.

As Rabbi Joseph Telushkin wrote,

> I sometimes wonder if, by attributing the book to Solomon, the rabbis were exacting a gentle revenge on the ancient Jewish monarch. For while Jewish tradition regards him as the wisest man who ever lived, the Bible makes it clear that in his final years Solomon became a bit of a fool and an arrogant one at that. Thus, in attributing Ecclesiastes to Solomon's last years, perhaps the rabbis were delivering a "hidden," if ironic, assessment of their true feelings about the value of this work.[2]

The reign of Solomon led to the golden era of Israel, with the temple being built and envoys from around the nation coming to marvel at its prosperity and Solomon's wisdom. His legacy left an abundance of buildings, writings, and riches. But as his meditations in Ecclesiastes warned, "If a man fathers a hundred children and lives many years, so that the days of his years are many, but his soul is not satisfied with life's good things, and he also has no burial, I say that a stillborn child is better off than he" (6:3).

If Solomon reflected on his life, some memories would sting. Comic Billy Crystal once quipped that "By the time a man is wise enough to watch his step, he's too old to go anywhere." An old man's back goes out more than he does. Old Solomon didn't go out much, but he stewed over and rued his own history. His father's most notorious sin was to abduct and seduce Solomon's mother, Bathsheba, Uriah's wife. What kind of odd and uncomfortable moment occurred when Solomon first asked his father with gleeful curiosity, "Dad, how did you meet Mom?"

Toward the ends of Solomon's life, he taxed and enslaved his own people to raise money for the construction of the temple in

Jerusalem. He left behind a son who threatened his own followers, and soon afterward we see the kingdom dividing into Israel and Judah. Solomon left little wisdom for his son Rehoboam. When Rehoboam became king, there were some older men who had once helped Solomon make decisions. King Rehoboam asked them what he should do in answering the people, and they offered wisdom. They counseled him to be a servant to his people, speaking good words to them and thus receiving their loyalty. Instead, Rehoboam forsook their wisdom and listened to his friends, the young punks who told him to make the people's yoke heavier. They told him to tell the people, "My little finger is thicker than my father's loins. Instead of disciplining you with whips, I will discipline you with scorpions."

Solomon had good reason to be cynical in his old age. His folly would pass on, with a double portion given to his offspring.

Throughout his life, Solomon increasingly had a worldview that did not include God. His wisdom had become meaningless to him. His construction projects included not only the temple in Jerusalem but also shrines and temples to other gods. As an old man of the Bible, Solomon lived a life that had become so encased in cynicism that he lost any sense of meaning.

The message of Ecclesiastes may stand out in at least one positive way. There may be nothing new "under the sun," but as people of faith, we need to recognize that God—who is not "under the sun"— brings deeper meaning to every aspect of our lives. Solomon reminds us of how dark and foolish a life can end if it is not rooted in God.

For Discussion and Further Reflection

1. When you think of Solomon, what stands out most about him? Is there anything not mentioned here?

2. What stood out to you in this chapter?

3. Have you ever read the Song of Songs or Ecclesiastes? Are you interested in doing so now . . . or not so much?

4. Eyes like doves, hair like goats, cheeks like pomegranates: these metaphors may not resonate with women today, but they clearly spoke to women in the past. Think of wives, sisters, or other women in your life. What would they like to hear that you don't say frequently enough? What kind of support or compliments would they appreciate?

5. Solomon's many marriages likely grew out of political alliances and a desire for good relations with other countries. However, the marriages ended up leading Solomon further away from God. Think about aspects of your life and relationships that grow out of good intentions but lead you away from God.

6. There is no mention of God in the Song of Solomon. In what situations do you fail to include God or your faith?

7. The author of Ecclesiastes unsuccessfully tried to find meaning in his possessions, laughter, entertainment, wisdom, and even wine, but nothing satisfied him. None of it helped. Sometimes it is easy to be world weary and not find meaning anywhere. What do you do in those moments? How can you turn to God? When God seems too abstract, where can you find meaning?

Notes

1. Thomas Cathcart and Daniel Klein, *Plato and a Platypus Walk into a Bar: Understanding Philosophy through Jokes* (New York: Abrams Image, 2007) 8–9.

2. Joseph Telushkin, *Biblical Literacy: The Most Important People, Events, and Ideas of the Hebrew Bible* (New York: William Morrow and Company, Inc., 1997) 367.

Chapter 9

The Pride of Hezekiah

Psalm 90:10 announces that the "years of our life are seventy, or even by reason of strength eighty; yet their span is but toil and trouble; they are soon gone, and we fly away." It is not a good announcement, but it alerts us to our present predicament. We can't say we haven't been warned.

In his *Pints and Parables* series, British storyteller Peter Rollins retells an ancient Islamic parable about a worker's date with death. A merchant sends his worker into the market of Baghdad. Finishing his shopping and making his way through the crowd, the worker bumps into a person dressed in black. As the person turns around, he looks shocked to see the worker and points a menacing hand at him.

The terrified worker realizes the person is Death and runs back to the merchant to tell him what happened. "What can I do?" asks the worker.

"Take my fastest horse and ride as quickly as you can to the city of Samaara and hide in my house. I will go and take care of this person." The worker flees immediately while the merchant goes down to the marketplace and sees Death.

He walks up to him and confronts him, saying, "What were you doing scaring my worker?"

Death responds, "I wasn't trying to scare him. I was just surprised to find him here buying supplies for you. I was supposed to meet him tonight in Samaara, and I was supposed to meet you here in the marketplace."

For every season, there is a time to be born and a time to die. It is appointed for a man to come to his grave at a full, mature age, just as a shock of corn ripens in its proper season. When full age comes, it is time. One has an appointment with death, either in Samaara or Virginia Beach.

The length of our lives is fully dependent on the grace of God, but Moses also indicated that we could live a long time if we obeyed the Ten Commandments. The fifth commandment, in particular, promises that if you obey your parents, you may receive the blessings of a long and fruitful life. When you are in your sixties and above, that duty is often not available.

But it seems that God is open to negotiate. Sometimes the good die young (as most of us who are old will testify when we look at who is left). Most of the time, we don't get a hearing to barter with God, but that doesn't mean it can't happen. And even when it happens, we can't be too sure that it is wise to barter in this way. When death comes, however, one can sing with the psalmist that "Precious in the sight of the LORD is the death of his servants."

When he was twenty-five years old, Hezekiah became king of Judah. He reigned for twenty-nine years and did right in the sight of the Lord. He clung to the Lord and kept the commandments. He called the Levites to consecrate themselves and the house of the Lord, ridding the holy place of uncleanness. What a great beginning in his youth.

Later on, he would squeeze some extra years from God. Hezekiah liked the first two acts of his life, but he requested that the Great Scriptwriter revise the third act. Those last years, however, would not be as blessed as the first; old age would expose some creeping tendencies to bloviate a bit, to puff up his achievements with a little arrogance.

Death would come to Hezekiah inevitably. Everyone has an appointment with death (except for old Enoch and Elijah, who had good lawyers).

Two elderly Boston Red Sox fans named Moe and Sam had spent their lives going to every game and waxed eloquent about the 2013 World Series. But one August, Moe died suddenly in the seventh-inning stretch of a game against the Yankees. Sam was inconsolable.

That night, Moe appeared to Sam as he sat drooling over his beer. "I have some good news and some bad news," he told Sam.

"Heaven's great!" Moe said. "We have baseball 24/7 and it's always extra innings."

"Wow!" said Sam. "But what's the bad news?"

Moe said, "You're pitching tomorrow."

No one is ever ready to go, even when one wants to go.

In the beginning, Hezekiah crushed the sacred pillars, cut down the Asherah, and even destroyed the archival bronze serpent of Moses when the Israelites began worshiping it. This serpent, Nehushton, had once symbolized the healing God had brought to the people, but now, situated in the temple court, many burned incense to the bronze serpent superstitiously. Hezekiah went further with the zeal of youth, calling for a renewed covenant with the Lord and cleansing the house of the Lord, including the altar of burnt offerings, the table of showbread, and all the utensils. When all was washed and cleaned, Hezekiah brought bulls, rams, lambs, and male goats (seven of each at first) and made sin offerings for the people, slaughtering the animals and sprinkling their blood to purge the place. Then, with cymbals, harps, lyres, a few trumpets, and one electric guitar, they all offered songs and music in worship. Joy overwhelmed them (2 Chron 29:15-19).

This early reign of Hezekiah was an ongoing celebration, with a decree to remember and celebrate the Passover—the Feast of Unleavened Bread—and a warning to the people not to stiffen their necks. One has a tendency to get uppity, to get as stubborn as an ox when all is going your way. In the midst of a party, one easily might forget to be guided by God, especially if the wine is flowing freely. But the people came in humility and faithfully brought their tithes. Even those who had not been properly consecrated themselves were pardoned, as Hezekiah interceded: "May the good Lord pardon everyone who prepares his heart to seek God, even if not by a strict reading of the rules." The Lord heard and the party continued.

Now, with such festive noise, the dreaded Assyrians heard and decided to invade Judah. The Assyrian leader, Sennacherib, besieged fortified cities. Hezekiah bargained with the Assyrians, offering gold from the doors and doorposts of the temple, trying vainly to mollify the aggression. The people of the northern kingdom of Israel had been carried off to captivity, and now Hezekiah had to face an onslaught of brutal force.

When the chief Assyrian vizier Rabshakeh arrived, he lambasted the stubborn people of Jerusalem for not capitulating to the great army. He told the people not to listen to Hezekiah, as he was misleading them, nor let him make them trust in the Lord whom he promised would deliver them. "Look," Rabshakeh said, "he took away your high altars"—not understanding that these altars were a stench to Jehovah.

The Jewish leaders asked that he speak in Aramaic and not Hebrew, but Rabshakeh scorned them and said, "No way!" He wanted to terrorize them: "I'm talking to the men who sit on the wall—those doomed to eat their own dung and drink their own urine."

"But come over to the Assyrian side," he gently cajoled. "Make peace with me, come on out, and eat each of his own vine and each of his own fig tree and drink each of the water of his own cistern." Seductively, he spuriously promised, "Come to me and I will take you away to a land like your own land, a land of bread and vineyards, olive trees and honey." It was tempting to follow him, but the people obediently stayed silent.

Hezekiah tore his clothes, put on his best, or worst, sackcloth, and entered the house of the Lord on this day of distress and darkness. The words of Isaiah strengthened him and encouraged him not to fear, as it was the Lord who had been blasphemed. The Lord would make sure the Assyrians fell by the sword in their own land.

"Because you have prayed to me," the Lord told Hezekiah, "I have heard you." The need of the young king kept him humble before the Lord.

Now the people Assyria blasphemed God, despising, mocking, and shaking their heads with haughtily raised voice and the sneering lift of their eyes. The Lord found this boasting to be a bit much: "Because your arrogance has come up to my ears, I will put my hook in your nose and my bridle in your lips." And God meant it literally. What the Assyrians had done to the northern kingdom would be done to them.

So the Lord defended the city, reaffirming his servant Hezekiah. Striking 185,000 warriors in the camp, the Lord's angel of death wiped out every mighty warrior and commander. He chased

Sennacherib back to Nineveh, with his tail between his legs, straight into the house of his god Nisroch. Nisroch was depicted as an eagle-headed human figure with wings and exaggerated muscles and was associated with a special plank of wood allegedly from Noah's ark, which Sennacherib worshipped. Isaiah would mock such wooden idols: "Ah, you make your god and your stool out of the same material" (Isa 44:13-19). According to *The Onion*, this forgotten Assyrian god of agriculture or the moon was revived as a sleek marketing label for a Powerade sports drink, bringing supernatural electrolyte replenishment for waning athletes, supplying X-TREME WHIRLWIND energy.[1] No such awesome power existed for Sennacherib, who was assassinated by two of his own sons as he knelt before the big bird.

So Hezekiah felt emboldened and ready to party again.

But then he got sick. The battle had been stressful, and he was getting older. He was told to put his house in order, as it was time to die, but he decided to cry and entreat God. He realized that old age wasn't so bad when you considered the alternative.

Our comedians have always given us perspective on being old. Will Rogers, the man who never met a man he didn't like, suggested we could "certainly slow the aging process down if it had to work its way through Congress." So, too, holding his cigar, actor George Burns reminisced, "When I was a boy, the Dead Sea was only sick." He continued, "At my age, flowers scare me."

Hezekiah didn't want to die yet. He pleaded and schemed to get some extra minutes in the game. He was like the last of three old men who were asked by their minister what they wanted him to say at their funerals. The first said, "Remember my faith, my devotion to my family, my generosity to others." The second asked if the minister would tell all the comic things he had done in his life. The third said he wanted the minister to look at his body in the coffin and proclaim, "My God, he's moving!"

God took pity on Hezekiah's tears and healed him, adding fifteen years to his life and a holiday up in Gilgal if he wanted it. His doctors took a cake of figs and laid it on his festering boil and he recovered, but Hezekiah wanted to make sure this wasn't just a scam so he asked Isaiah for a sign.

"Okay," said the prophet, "you want that a shadow should go backwards ten steps or forward ten steps when you are on the stairway?" "Oh, backwards," replied Hezekiah, as he thought it might look cool.

With the promise of an old age and a wild shadow, Hezekiah should have been content to tend his people and laugh about Sennacherib. But instead, he got a bit proud, provoking the wrath of the Lord. He began to accumulate such riches that had not been known since the days of Solomon.

ISAIAH, FIFTEEN YEARS IS GREAT BUT COULD YOU SEE IF HE'D DO TWENTY?

Visited by a son of the king of Babylon, who was bringing a get-well card and a gift, perhaps a little magic dragon from Marduk, Hezekiah wanted to show off his treasures: gold, silver, spices, precious oil, a house of armor, shields, cattle, and probably some knick-knack souvenirs from Egypt including a stuffed cat. There was nothing in his house or in all his dominion that Hezekiah did not show his visitors. Hezekiah had great wealth. Very great wealth. He had made Judah great again. It prospered materially. It was great.

"What's up?" Isaiah asked. "What did these visitors from Babylon see?"

"Everything," bragged the old man. "My retirement accounts, my best camels. There is nothing among my treasuries that I have not shown them."

"Wait a minute, old man," barked Isaiah, who rarely got angry like other prophets. "Hear the word of the Lord. I am giving it all to

Babylon. Your sons, whom you shall beget [well, there is some good news here] shall serve in Babylon."

Hezekiah thought to himself, "Hey, this is good. For there will be peace and truth and no global warming in all *my* days!" So he went about doing some good things, like making a pool and a conduit and bringing water into the city. But his undisciplined old age, his talent for showing off, blunted the future for his children.

In old age, we tend to see our lives in golden hues. Our victories seem larger; our failures forgotten. We brag of those mini-moments of glory and see them as the fulcrum that leveraged the world. Hezekiah couldn't help but show off.

Finally, he slept with his fathers, serenely we hope. But his son Manasseh became king and did evil in the sight of the Lord according to all the pagan abominations, the Baals and the Asherim. All the good of Hezekiah came to naught, as he hadn't spent time with the legacy that counted most: Manasseh. But at least they had running water.

The desire to live longer may tempt some old men. Hezekiah's desire to extend his life, even to do good works, brought with it a duty to live that life more righteously. Along with aging, though, comes the foolishness of old men who tend to boast and exaggerate. Let us not try to extend this life too much, lest we increase folly.

A man watching a program on medical technology and life extension told his wife that if he ever became dependent on a machine, his wife was to pull the plug. The wife got up and unplugged the TV. Someone should have pulled the plug on Hezekiah a little earlier.

God answers prayers. The problem is, even in the age of wisdom we don't always know how to pray. James pointed to the fact that we ask and do not receive because we ask amiss (James 4:3). Sometimes God answers our prayers, but the irony is that it isn't what we wanted, or, if we had known what would happen, we might have stepped back and said to God, "Thy will be done."

For Discussion and Further Reflection

1. What did you know about Hezekiah before reading this chapter?

2. What stood out to you in this chapter?

3. What do you hope to do in your later years to bring glory to God and deep meaning to your life? What paths do you recognize you could take but hope to avoid?

4. Reflect on the individuals you know who have lived lives filled with meaning as they have aged. What do they have in common? What would be good to emulate from them?

Note

1. "Forgotten Assyrian God Revived to Name Sports Drink," TheOnion.com, February 13, 2010, www.theonion.com/ forgotten-assyrian-god-revived-to-name-sports-drink-1819571316.

Chapter 10

The Sharpness of Paul

As one who wrote numerous letters while chained in prison, the apostle Paul left behind words that inspired Christians during the worst of persecutions. As the author of many letters, his name is attributed to almost half (thirteen out of twenty-seven) of the writings of the New Testament. And as the apostle to the Gentiles, Paul created the conditions for the church to flourish long after Jewish interest waned.

He was not always seen in such a light. When he first appears in Acts 7:58, the Pharisee Saul is holding others' coats—apparently freeing up their arms—as they are stoning Stephen, the deacon who would come to be known as the first Christian martyr. A few verses later Saul is described as ravaging churches and dragging Christian men and women into prison. Less law enforcement and more bounty hunter, Saul quickly came to have a reputation and a name that was feared.

So when he was blinded on a business trip to Damascus, when his Christian hunting expedition was cut short by his inability to go further, when the brilliance of the risen Christ appeared to him and left him blinded, it is no surprise that Christians still feared him and wanted to keep him at a distance.

On the road to Damascus, the risen Christ appeared to Paul and confronted him with the question, "Why do you persecute my people?" The net result was Saul's being incapacitated by blindness.

The story of Saul's being blinded on the road to Damascus is so significant that it is repeated three times in the book of Acts, each in a slightly different manner. The story is significant for the development of Christianity—as Saul the persecutor became Paul the apostle—that *odos*, the Greek word for "road" or "way," became the first name for the Christian religion. Only later, in Antioch, would the faith come to be known as Christianity.

But first, still on the road and still blind, Saul had no place to go. The evangelist Luke, the author of the book of Acts, notes in Acts 19 that the Lord appeared to Ananias and told him that Saul had converted and that Ananias should go help and retrieve him. Ananias responded with incredulity. Probably nausea.

But it all worked out, and life changed: Saul, the persecutor of Christians, came to be known as Paul, the apostle.

We change our names for all sorts of reasons. Marriage traditionally has led women to change their last names, adopting that of their husband. Faith led the boxer Cassius Clay to embrace the name Muhammad Ali. Perhaps a desire for uniqueness or a desire to write fewer letters was what led some individuals, like Elvis, Prince, or Madonna, to adopt a new name (or also a new glyph, in Prince's case).

It is not clear what motivations Saul had. Likely his new name signaled a new beginning. As he became an evangelist to Greek-speaking Gentiles, perhaps he thought a new name was in order. The word "Paul" comes from a Roman family name that means "small." Perhaps he chose to be known as Paul because he was sufficiently humbled by Jesus' appearance to him and recognized how little he was against God.

In his book *The Psalms*, James Johnston recounts this story about Teddy Roosevelt and naturalist William Beebe:

> At Sagamore Hill, after talking for the evening, the two would go out on the lawn and search the skies for a certain star-like light near the lower left-hand corner of the Great Square of Pegasus. Roosevelt would recite: "That is the Spiral Galaxy in Andromeda. It is as large as our Milky Way. It is one of a hundred million galaxies. It consists of one hundred billion suns, each larger than our sun." Then Roosevelt would grin and say, "Now I think we are small enough! Let's go to bed."[1]

Paul, however, certainly didn't always see himself in such humble ways. In Philippians 3, as he looks back on who he had been before he was called to serve Christ, he describes himself as one who had all sorts of reasons to boast. This Jew from Tarsus, who studied at the feet of the rabbi Gamaliel in Jerusalem, recognized that he had an impressive résumé. In Philippians 3:4-6 he writes, "If anyone else has reason to be confident in the flesh, I have more: circumcised on the eighth day, a member of the people of Israel, of the tribe of Benjamin, a Hebrew born of Hebrews; as to the law, a Pharisee; as to zeal, a persecutor of the church; as to righteousness under the law, blameless."

Paul didn't see himself as just great. He saw himself as so much greater than everyone else.

His attitude is like that of an associate pastor in one of my favorite stories of spiritual arrogance.

A local church pastor, burdened by the importance of his work, went into the sanctuary to pray. Falling to his knees, he lamented, "O Lord, I am nothing! I am nothing."

The minister of education passed by and, overhearing the prayer, was moved to join the pastor on his knees. Shortly he, too, was crying aloud, "O Lord, I too am nothing. I am nothing."

The janitor of the church, awed by the sight of the two men praying, joined them, crying, "O Lord, I also am nothing. I am nothing." At this the minister of education nudged his senior pastor and said, "*Now* look who thinks *he's* nothing!"[2]

While Paul wrote a lot about putting off the old man and putting on the new, he still used the pronoun "I" quite a bit. But we learn valuable lessons from such a man. Despite his opinionated rhetoric, he did believe in Someone greater than himself. He knew he couldn't just believe in himself. It got him nowhere.

Chesterton once told of an encounter with a prestigious publisher who casually remarked that so and so was a man who believed in himself. He had raised himself up by his own bootstraps. Seeing a bus drive by with an advertisement for a mental hospital, Chesterton retorted that he knew where all the men who truly believed in themselves congregated.[3]

Saul came to be called Paul likely because it was a name that made sense to him. He came to see himself as small, as a servant, as a cog, as a player in God's story, not as the lead in his own story. This is particularly clear in Philippians 3. After he states the reasons he had been so great (vv. 4-6), he then says in verse 8 that he has come to see all of these qualifications as nothing more than "rubbish" or worthless. The actual Greek word probably should be translated more strongly than "rubbish." Some Bibles use the word "dung," But the Greek word that Paul uses here—*skublion*—would be better translated with the word "poop" (or something grosser and more scatological). Paul knows that everything he has previously bragged about isn't all that important. Particularly not in God's eyes.

After he persecuted the church, after he was blinded, Paul traveled, sharing the gospel with the Gentiles of his day, particularly in the areas that we know today as Turkey and Greece. Paul was from Tarsus, but from both the book of Acts and Paul's own letters, we can see that he was on the road a great deal. In Acts, Paul travels more than 10,000 miles.

Because of his profession, he could travel lightly. He had a trade (1 Thess 2:9; 1 Cor 4:12); officially he was a tentmaker. And just as cabinetmakers today don't make only cabinets but engage in all sorts of carpentry, so tentmakers in Paul's day didn't make only tents but also made any items made of leather: saddles, stirrups, water jugs, clothing, and the like. With a few tools, he could travel lightly. And he met people, and he evangelized, while he worked.

It is easy to imagine Paul working alone, but if we read the Bible, we know that all sorts of people worked with him. He had his faithful sidekicks, Timothy and Titus, who served him with the kind of allegiance characteristic of figures like Tonto, Sancho Panza, and Ed McMahon. Onesimus and Epaphroditus were with Paul for at least a season. Barnabas had been an important part of his ministry. And then Paul, throughout his letters, mentions good friends and colleagues like Chloe (1 Cor 1:11), Phoebe (Rom 16:1), Euodia, Syntyche, and Clement (Phil 4:2-3), and—at the end of his letter to the Romans—twenty-six people from the city of Rome. What is so remarkable is that he had not yet visited Rome. These were all people he had met through his traveling.

Over the course of a long life—more than sixty years—Paul had worked with many people. In describing how Paul could be identified by those who were waiting for him, the second-century writing *The Acts of Paul* (*The Martyrdom of Thecla* 3) shares a physical description. It is the most complete physical description we have of any New Testament figure. The writing says that Paul was "a man small in size, with a bald head and crooked legs; in good health; with eyebrows that met and a rather prominent nose."

Although the description may not sound flattering, professors Abraham Malherbe and Robert Grant note that this description was intended to be so. It mirrors a well-known description from the ancient writer Archilochus, who describes the ideal kind of general: "I love not a tall general nor one long-shanked, nor with splendid curls or partly sheared. Let me have one who is short and bow-legged, firm on his feet, full of heart."[4]

The ideal general is small, stable, and not concerned with his hair. He has other things to focus on.

Thus, when Paul is described, it seems he is portrayed as one who resembles a general. The description in *The Acts of Paul* may not be accurate; it may simply be used in sparking the imagination of the readers. If we take the description of Paul and subtract all the ways in which a good general was characterized, we are left with a man with two distinctive features: a unibrow and a prominent nose.

That might be the only thing we know for sure about how Paul looked.

Paul was described as "a general of God." He certainly led many people, and he certainly had strong opinions. As a Pharisee, he had been a zealous persecutor of the church, but just because he was no longer persecuting the church didn't mean he had lost his zeal.

We can see him aging in the text of his letters. His deep frustration sometimes spills from his pen. Not only did he identify himself as a prisoner of Jesus Christ when he wrote Philemon; he also called himself "the aged." He pointed out that he did not want to compel Philemon to let Onesimus free, but then he offered a quick reminder that Philemon owed his life to Paul (Philemon 19).

And when Paul wrote to the church in Corinth, instructing them on how to take part in the Lord's Supper, he made fun of the fact that some people ate before others—thereby undermining the sacrament. As he said, "Indeed, there have to be factions among you, for only so will it become clear who among you are genuine" (1 Cor 11:19).

And, when he was frustrated with the Galatians, he wrote words that didn't equip them or build them up as much as they were intended to rip into them. The English word "sarcasm" comes from the Greek word "sarx," which means "flesh." Sarcasm literally means "ripping of flesh," and that is what Paul did in writing the Galatians. He was beyond frustrated with those who called themselves followers of Christ and who had preached to the Galatians, telling them that they needed to be circumcised in order to be true Christ followers. Paul's response to them in Galatians 5:12 has been translated in a variety of ways, each one harsh: "So then, what about troublemakers who try to get others to be circumcised? I wish they would go the whole way! I wish they would cut off everything that marks them as men!" (NIRV); "As for those agitators, I wish they would go the whole way and emasculate themselves!" (NIV).

In that same letter, Paul wrote, "You foolish Galatians! Who has bewitched you?" (Gal 3:1), and he uncharacteristically left out of the beginning of the letter any kind of thanksgiving for them. However much his harshness and righteous indignation may have felt justified, it is sad to see—in Romans 15:26—that the Galatians ended up being the one group who did not contribute money for the saints in Jerusalem. Whatever else Paul's words did, in his letter to the Galatians they ended up separating the people of Galatia from Paul.

With deep concern and deep love for those whom he was trying to guide in the faith, Paul could be impassioned and zealous. At times he could also be sarcastic and filled with righteous indignation. His words could be sharp and cutting. And, although he shared his words in love, we know that they pushed some people away from the gospel that he so sincerely wanted to share. Paul had the last word, and it could be a word that drove people away.

As cranky old men—even with all the good we do and all the love we have—sometimes we try to have the last word. Or we send letters or messages before thinking about what we want to accomplish by sharing them. Or when we are tired, emotional, or frustrated, unintentionally using wrong words that push away those we love the most. But there is a better way, and Paul himself reminded us of it. In his letter to the Ephesians, Paul calls on Christians to "speak the truth in love" (4:15) and to avoid "obscene, silly, and vulgar talk" (5:4). All of this is to be done in order "to equip the saints for the work of ministry, for building up the body of Christ" (4:12). Our prayer should not be that we are silent, but that in all we do we seek to share words that heal and that build up the body of Christ. The rest we can leave to God.

For Discussion and Further Reflection

1. When you think of Paul, what stands out most about him? Is there anything not mentioned here?

2. What stood out to you in this chapter?

3. The Lord appeared to Ananias and told him to reach out to Saul, the notorious Christian hunter. Ananias was understandably reluctant. When do you see Christians who are reluctant to reach out to others? We know that we should reach out to all people and offer them good invitations into the life of the church, but sometimes we are reluctant to invite everyone. Why? Who?

4. Paul came to see himself as "little." He was not the lead actor in a drama; he simply played a role. Why is humility important in God's world?

5. When are you too sharp and cutting with your speech? What might you do to prevent that? Who is someone whom you respect who always seems to use measured words or thought-filled language in their interactions with others? Why is their approach effective?

Notes

1. James A. Johnston, *The Psalms, Vol. 1: Psalms 1–41: Rejoice, the Lord is King* (Preaching the Word; Wheaton IL: Crossway, 2015).

2. Paul M. Miller, comp., *World's Greatest Collection of Church Jokes* (Uhrichsville OH: Barbour Publishing, 2003).

3. G. K. Chesterton, *Orthodoxy* (San Francisco: Ignatius Press, 1986) 216.

4. Robert M. Grant, "The Description of Paul in the Acts of Paul and Thecla," *Vigiliae Christianae* 36/1 (1982): 1–4. doi:10.2307/1583027.

The Grace of God Redux

In the last days, God says, I will pour out my Spirit on all people.
Your sons and daughters will prophesy, your young men will see
visions, your old men will dream dreams. (Acts 2:17)

Those who are planted in the house of the LORD
shall flourish in the courts of our God;
They shall still bear fruit in old age; they shall be green and
succulent;
That they may show how upright the LORD is,
my Rock, in whom there is no fault. (Psalm 92:12-14)

We've reached the end of the book, and we are all older. Time
slipped by, didn't it? But, Lord willing and clock ticking, we may all
have a few more hours left in this old body. Perhaps we are like the
old man who fell off a cliff and, as he was plummeting to the earth,
muttered, "So far, so good."

Listening to Pete Docter, the Pixar director of the films *Monsters,
Inc.*, *Up*, and *Inside Out*, talk about old people and things they do—
avoiding spicy foods, chewing with their mouths open, and getting
grouchy—one realizes that we are remarkably interesting. If only
young people could look at us with the curiosity of seeing a dinosaur,
who knows what they might experience? But we learn this as we age,
not understanding it when we are young.

Many other biblical characters offer us perspectives on aging.
Uzziah, like the men in this book, offer negative warnings. When
Uzziah was made king at sixteen, things looked great and he would
remain king for fifty-two years: "And he did right in the sight of the
Lord . . . as long as he sought the Lord" (2 Chron 26:4, 5). However,
he became so proud that he acted corruptly, so presumptuous that
he entered the temple of the Lord to burn incense. He was like that

angry old man who yells at kids to get off his lawn. But Azariah, the priest, opposed him and said that only the consecrated sons of Aaron were to burn incense.

"Phooey!" spit out an enraged Uzziah.

Suddenly, he was smitten by God and leprosy broke out on his forehead. "And King Uzziah was a leper to the day of his death; and he lived in a separate house," living apart from the house of the Lord and his people (2 Chron 26:21).

A stubborn streak, an irate temper, or a haughty spirit can sneak up upon even a good man as he ages. Uzziah's mark of physical leprosy exposed a spiritual arrogance in which he did not feel that God's law applied to kings.

However, other old men provide wisdom, hope, and comfort. Jethro, Moses' father-in-law, offered him great advice to lessen the strain of his work. He saw how much Moses did for all the people and asked, "Why do you along sit and hear people mutter all day? The thing you do is not good. You're going to wear yourself out." So, in his wisdom, he counseled Moses to select good men to judge the people, to share in the dispensing of justice. An old father-in-law can be helpful (Exod 18:1-27).

Waiting, waiting, waiting: both Zechariah and Simeon waited for the Messiah. Zechariah was "well advanced in years" when his wife Elizabeth got pregnant. When he doubted Gabriel, the angel who announced this miracle, Zechariah wasn't allowed to speak for months until he named his son. But when he did speak, he prophesied with power and poetry the blessing of the Lord to give light to those who dwell in darkness (Luke 1:79).

Being old, Simeon had no filter to control his speech. After seeing and blessing Mary's holy child, he was ready to depart in peace, having encountered the Consolation of Israel. But then, like an old guy, he blurted out to the new mother Mary, "And a spear will pierce your own soul too" (Luke 2:35). Couldn't he have waited to say this?

We are stuck between two moments of last days. First, we read Ecclesiastes 12 about grinding our teeth in the years when we no longer have the delight in our youth, when the sun, the moon, and the stars are darkened, when mighty men stoop and grinding ones stand idle. This concern echoes Psalm 71, in which the writer worries whether his family will cast him off in the time of old age. His cry becomes "forsake me not when my strength is spent."

Here we may be kin to Statler and Waldorf, that cantankerous pair of elderly Muppet characters who sit in the balcony and kvetch and heckle. They spend their few precious moments on *The Muppet Show* jeering at the entirety of the cast from their elevated perch. Named after the great New York City hotels, the Waldorf-Astoria and the Statler Hilton, the two old monuments to irascible behavior let people know what they think. After one brief absence, the two curmudgeons reappear and one says, "It's good to be heckling again."

The other replies in true old-man fashion, "It's good to be doing *anything* again!" When the first boasts that they got their money's worth for the show that night, his partner quips, "But we paid nothing." To which the first retorts, "That's what we got!"

The second response is to remember the days of old. As the psalmist sang, "I meditate on all your doings; I muse on the work of your hands." (Ps 143:5). If we have even a few mental faculties, we may gladly spend our thoughts on the blessings of God. But if we have not been practicing thanksgiving, we may now know how to learn. Perhaps we can't teach an old dog new tricks, but we must try to learn.

Swiss psychologist Paul Tournier wrote of hearing a story about old men in (an unnamed country in) Africa in which "the men . . . gather every day for several hours in the village square—their own Agora."[1] Asked what they talk about, he said that they argue about the "meaning of life and death, the meaning of sickness and health." Like the ancient Greeks in their agora and Hebrews sitting in the gates of the city, these men gather and tell the old stories to make sense of it all.

Albert Camus's exploration of the myth of Sisyphus concerns the mythical hero whom Zeus condemned to push an enormous boulder up a steep hill, only to see it roll back to the bottom again as he reached the peak. Are all such struggles of life so repetitively futile and so frustrating? Is there no meaning to life?

All men are on the edge of the eternal. The eternal life has already begun, and we are trekking either up or down. Even if we feel like Sisyphus, we keep falling.

Perhaps, other than the Scriptures, it is fitting to let the old Muppet pair have the penultimate words.

> *Statler:* I guess all's well that ends well.
> *Waldorf:* Doesn't matter to me, as long as it ends.
> *Waldorf:* Just when you think the show is terrible, something wonderful happens.
> *Statler:* What?
> *Waldorf:* It ends.

The psalmist tells us, probably with a wink and a bit of a smile, that the righteous shall "still bear fruit in old age; they may still be ever full of sap and green" (or, to put it more encouragingly, we shall be fat, fresh, and flourishing in our old age; Ps 92:14). Whether bald or adorned with gray hair, we receive a crown of glory.

Awaiting that crown, whether it be of gold, paper, or thorns, comes a call for a palinode, basically a retraction of much that we've written. Toby Keith composed the lyrics for a song in eighty-eight-year-old director Clint Eastwood's 2018 film, *The Mule*, titled "Don't Let the Old Man In." Just before Eastwood was to begin directing, he and Keith were playing golf for a charity tournament in Pebble Beach, California. When Keith inquired about how this living legend was still able to function so marvelously, Eastwood quipped, "I just get up every morning and go out. And I don't let the old man in." The musician knew he had inspiration for a country song. It also works as a biblical parable.

> Don't let the old man in, I wanna leave this alone
> Can't leave it up to him, he's knocking on my door
> And I knew all of my life, that someday it would end
> Get up and go outside, don't let the old man in
> Many moons I have lived
> My body's weathered and worn

Ask yourself how old you'd be
If you didn't know the day you were born

Try to love on your wife
And stay close to your friends
Toast each sundown with wine
Don't let the old man in.

The lyrics unintentionally point back to St. Paul's distinction of the old man and the new man in his letters (Rom 6:6; Eph 2:15, 4:22-24; Col 3:9-11). Paul explains that our old man is crucified, that the life we shared with Adam in sin and death, has itself been put to death. That old man is dead. Why let him back in?

In Christ we have been made new men, men in relationship not only to God but to each other. God has creatively made us new men. Thus we are called to lay aside our old nature and enjoy ourselves as a new creation, renewing our minds and clothing ourselves with God's grace. Essentially we can put on fresh clothes and not have to wear the same old socks and boxer shorts. We are made new every day. And we're reminded, no matter how old we become, to enjoy the wife of our youth.

The book of Hebrews brings together some final thoughts on all these old men.

By faith Abraham obeyed when he was called to set out for a place that he was to receive as an inheritance; and he set out, not knowing where he was going. By faith he stayed for a time in the land he had been promised, as in a foreign land, living in tents, as did Isaac and Jacob, who were heirs with him of the same promise. For he looked forward to the city that has foundations, whose architect and builder is God. By faith he received power of procreation, even though he was too old—and Sarah herself was barren—because he considered God faithful who had promised. Therefore from one person, and this one as good as dead, descendants were born, "as many as the stars of heaven and as the innumerable grains of sand by the seashore" (Heb 11:12).

All of these died in faith without having received the promises, but from a distance they saw and greeted them. They confessed that they were strangers and foreigners on the earth, for people who speak in this way make it clear that they are seeking a homeland. If they had been thinking of the land that they had left behind, they would have had opportunity to return. But as it is, they desire a better country, that is, a heavenly one. Therefore God is not ashamed to be called their God; indeed, he has prepared a city for them.

And it is not an old folks' home or a retirement center.

Life ends like it began, not with a bang or a whimper but in grace. By faith, we are being prepared for a new youth. One of the first martyred saints of the young second-century church was the eighty-six-year-old Polycarp. Called before the pagan governor, he was commanded to renounce his faith. The proconsul tried to persuade him to deny Christ, saying, "Have regard for thine age," and "Swear by the genius of Caesar; repent and say, 'Away with the Atheists,'" for Christians were perceived as atheists since they believed in only one god.

> But Polycarp, looking with dignified countenance upon the whole crowd that was gathered in the stadium, waved his hand to them, and groaned, and raising his eyes toward heaven, said, "Away with the Atheists." But when the magistrate pressed him, and said, "Swear, and I will release thee; revile Christ," Polycarp said, "Four-score and six years have I been serving him, and he hath done me no wrong; how then can I blaspheme my king who saved me?"

As the proconsul persisted, Polycarp teased him, suggesting that the Roman might be ignorant of who he was: "Hear plainly: I am a Christian. But if you desire to learn the doctrine of Christianity, assign a day and hear." Basically, he was saying, "Let's have lunch and I will share my faith with you." Here was an old man with tremendous chutzpah!

Threatened with being burned alive, the witty Polycarp retorted, "You threaten with a fire which burns for an hour, and after a little is quenched; for you know not the fire of the future judgment and of the eternal punishment which is reserved for the impious. But why dost thou delay? Do what you will."

The eyewitness of the event records that after saying these words, Polycarp was "filled with courage and joy, and his face was suffused with grace."[2] It was grace at the end.

Polycarp had been a student of the beloved disciple John, a saint who seems to have aged as well as Moses. In his first epistle, John wrote to little children, young men, and older "fathers" who had known God from the beginning. The fathers had known God, who has been from the beginning. It was their knowledge of the love and grace of God that endured and enabled them to keep walking.

One apocryphal story of the disciple in his last days at Ephesus relates how the old disciple John would be brought up before the fellowship to speak. He would simply say, "Little children, love one another." For a long time, that was his only sermon. The younger men pleaded with him. He had known Jesus personally; he had been a beloved disciple; he had written about Jesus. They wondered what else he could tell besides, "Little children, love one another."

He responded, "When you have learned this, then I will tell you more. Little children, love one another."

The promise of God endures, longer than any of us. Through Isaiah, God called the people to listen. God calls all those who have been borne by him from their birth, even carried from the womb, that now in your old age, he is the one who will carry you, "even when you turn gray." He will carry and save (Isa 46:4).

As we mentioned in the beginning, old Father David Hubbard likewise gave his sermon: "Grace in the beginning, grace in the end, grace all the way through." It is a reminder to us all that, when we have learned this from these old men, we will be ready to hear more.

Notes

1. Paul Tournier, *Learn to Grow Old: A Doctor Reflects* (Eugene OR: Wipf & Stock, 1972) 129.

2. *Mart. Pol.* 25 (available at https://biblehub.com/library/pamphilius/church_history/chapter_xv_under_verus_polycarp_with.htm).

Made in the USA
Coppell, TX
17 March 2020